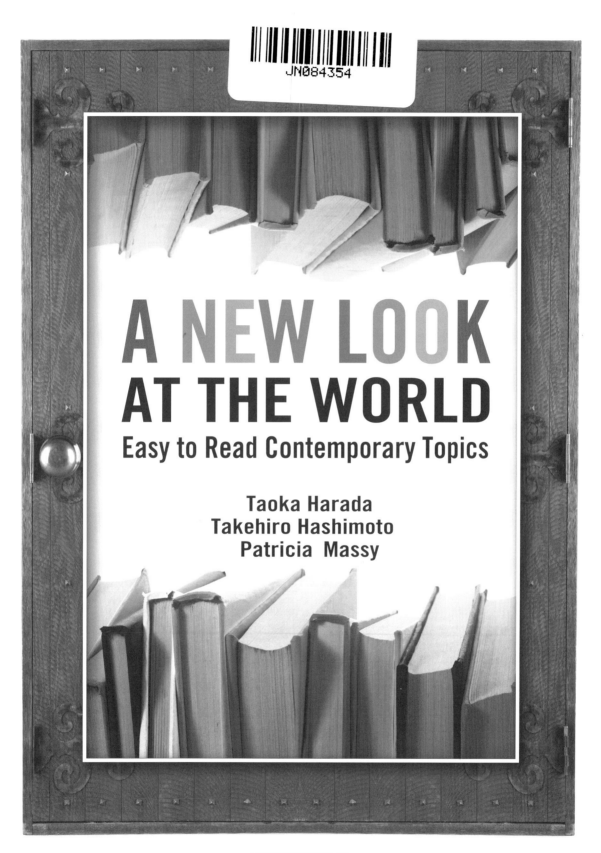

A NEW LOOK AT THE WORLD

Easy to Read Contemporary Topics

Taoka Harada
Takehiro Hashimoto
Patricia Massy

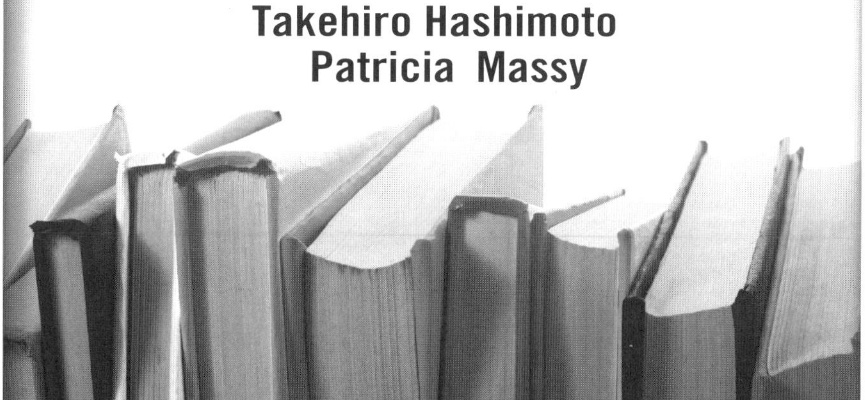

KINSEIDO

Kinseido Publishing Co., Ltd.
3-21 Kanda Jimbo-cho, Chiyoda-ku,
Tokyo 101-0051, Japan

First published 2020 by Kinseido Publishing Co., Ltd.

Cover design Takayuki Minegishi
Text design Yasuharu Yuki
Photo © Paul Prescott | Dreamstime.com (p.1, 2)
© J P | Dreamstime.com (p.19)
© Pniesen | Dreamstime.com (p.39)
© Rico Leffanta | Dreamstime.com (p.49)

音声ファイル無料ダウンロード

http://www.kinsei-do.co.jp/download/4104

4104

この教科書で DL 00 の表示がある箇所の音声は、上記 URL または QR コードにて無料でダウンロードできます。自習用音声としてご活用ください。

- ▶ PC からのダウンロードをお勧めします。スマートフォンなどでダウンロードされる場合は、**ダウンロード前に「解凍アプリ」をインストール**してください。
- ▶ URL は、**検索ボックスではなくアドレスバー（URL 表示欄）**に入力してください。
- ▶ お使いのネットワーク環境によっては、ダウンロードできない場合があります。

CD 00 左記の表示がある箇所の音声は、教室用 CD（Class Audio CD）に収録されています。

はじめに

辞書を引きながら英文を読むのは、すごく時間がかかる。それに知らない単語をすべて調べたけれど、話がよくわからない……。

長い英文の一語一語の意味を取っていくよりも、おおよその内容を理解することが大切——本テキストはそのようなにコンセプトのもとに作りました。題材となるのは、300 ワードくらいの短い英文で、シンプルでわかりやすい表現を用いています。そして、英語が苦手な人でも挫折しないように大半の問題を日本語で答えられるようにしました。取り上げるテーマは、映画やスポーツなど親しみやすいものから環境問題や貧困問題、ビジネスなど社会人向けのものまで多岐に渡り、語彙がシンプルでも読み応えのある内容になっています。

「すべてを読まなくてもおおよその内容を把握できる」読み方を身につけてもらうために、いきなり英文を読むことはしません。まずタイトルから内容を推測し、次に単語を見てその推測が当たっているかどうかをよく考えます。次に、段落内の重要な文だけを飛ばし読みし、話の流れをつかみます。このように十分に準備をした後で、単語の意味と文法表現を確認しながら英文を注意深く読みます。

今まで飛ばし読みをしたことがない人は、段落の一部を読むだけで内容を理解できるなんて信じられないかもしれませんが、まずは【本書の使い方について】に説明されているやり方を試してみてください。いくつかユニットを学習するうちに、知らない単語でも意味を予測できるようになり、一文ずつ順番に文章を訳していた時よりもずっと明確に内容が頭に入ることに気づくことでしょう。

【本書の使い方について】

LET'S START!

ここでは英文を読む前に、その内容を推測します。

Guess What?

まずユニットのタイトル、とくに斜字体で表記されている副題を手がかりにして、これから読む英文が何に関する話なのかを推測します。

Check Words

A. 本文中のキーワード・キーフレーズの意味を確認します。本文から抜き出した（一部は少しアレンジをしています）5つの文で、下線の語句の意味を推測します。そのあとで、文全体の意味を確認しましょう。

B. Aの5つの文の意味がわかったら、Guess What? で推測した内容と合致しているかどうかを考えます。

FIRST READING

まず英文を読むまえにページの右端にある「単語リスト」を見て、知っている単語にはチェックボックスに✓を入れます。知らない単語については、辞書を引かずに意味を推測してください。推測できない単語が半数以上あるときは、太字の文だけ単語を辞書で確認してください。

Paragraph Reading

ここで英文の読解に入ります。ただし、まだ全文は読まずに太字で書かれた文（各段落の内容を理解するためのキーとなる文です）だけを読み、その意味を推測します。

SECOND READING

Close Reading

FIRST READING で全体の内容を大体つかんだあとは、本文で使われた文法に焦点を当てます。ここに気をつけながらもう一度英文を読み直していくことで、内容の正しい理解につなげます。まず問題を解き、そのあとの解説で文法のポイントを確認します。

Reading Comprehension

選択肢の日本語の文が本文の内容に合っているかを問う問題です。選択肢が本文のどこについての記述かを探して線を引き、日本語の文の内容と一致する（あるいは一致しない）かを判断するとよいでしょう。

Listening

本文から抜き出した（一部アレンジ有り）3つの短い文を聞いて、その内容と一致するものを選ぶリスニング問題です。聞き取りに自信がない人は、Reading Comprehension と同じように日本語の文を読んでから、それと一致する文がありそうな段落を読み直してください。その後、音声を聞き、読まれた英文を見ながら答えると簡単にできるでしょう。聞き取りが得意な人は、この問題をやった後で、パッセージ全文を読んだ音声を聞いて、教科書を見ないで繰り返す練習にチャレンジしてみてください。

REFLECTION

ここまでに学んだ表現や文法を使って短い英文を作り、それを発話することで、応用力を養います。

Fill in the Blanks

英語では一語ずつはっきりと区切って発音せず二語、三語がくっついて発音されるために、まったく違う単語に聞こえることがあります。ここでは短い文を聞き、判別しづらい単語を書き取るトレーニングをします。音だけに頼らず、周りの単語との関連性もよく考えて空欄に入る単語を書いてみましょう。

Writing & Speaking

各ユニットの指示にしたがって、学んだ表現や文法を使って短い英文を作ります。英文が完成したらそれを暗記し、その後ペアを組んで、相手に向かって英文を発話します。これを繰り返すことで、英文とその基本構造を頭に叩き込みます。

書名の A New Look at the World とは、英語（英文読解）に対する見方を新たなものに変え、その視点で世界を見て（そして向き合って）ほしいという私たちの願いを表したものです。上記のエクササイズを通じて、英語の文章がより身近に、親しみのあるものになり、「もっと英語が読みたい」という気持ちになっていくことを心から願います。

著者一同

CONTENTS

Unit 1 Green School: *Where Learning Is Fun*

LET'S START!

Guess What?

"Green School: *Where Learning Is Fun*" というタイトルから何に関する文章を予想しますか。

a. 園芸を学ぶ学校

b. 緑色の校舎の学校

c. 自然の中で学べる楽しい学校

Check Words

A. 下線部の単語または語句の品詞に注意して、その意味をa～cから選びましょう。

1. They are completely open to the outdoors, so the breeze can pass through.
a. 風のような　**b.** 風が吹く　**c.** そよ風

2. The building is made entirely of bamboo.
a. 全体的に～製である　**b.** 部分的に～を作る　**c.** 絶対に～のメイドになる

3. Al Gore's movie tells about the dangers of global warming.
a. 傾向　**b.** 危険　**c.** 結果

4. John and Cynthia wanted children to learn to live in harmony with nature.
a. ハーモニーを奏でる　**b.** ～でハーモニカを吹く　**c.** ～と調和して

5. In a one-week Green Super Camp, the kids learn to live a sustainable life.
a. 持続可能な　**b.** ～を持続できる　**c.** 持続

B. 上の5つの文は本文に登場するものです。これらの意味から考えて、**Guess What?** で立てた予想は正しいですか。間違っていれば、選び直しましょう。

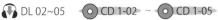

FIRST READING

DL 02~05　CD 1-02 ~ CD 1-05

英文を読み、あとに続く問題に答えなさい。

❶ **Green School doesn't look like a school. The classrooms have no walls.** They are completely open to the outdoors, so the breeze can pass through. The light is natural sunlight. The desks are not square. The building is made entirely of bamboo. Green School is in Bali, and 20% of the students are local Balinese children. The rest of the 160 students come from 25 countries around the world.

❷ **Green School was started in 2007 by John Hardy and his wife Cynthia.** They wanted children to enjoy learning. John himself had hated to go to school. He used to cry every day. He was dyslexic—that means he had trouble reading. Also, he had just seen the film *An Inconvenient Truth* by Al Gore. It tells about the dangers of global warming and the way human beings are causing it.

●●英文を読む前に●●

1. 知っている単語に ☑ を入れる
2. 【半数以上知っている】
→英文を読み、知らない単語の意味を類推する
【半数以上わからない】
→単語の意味を辞書で調べてから英文を読む

- ☐ completely
- ☐ outdoor
- ☐ to pass through
- ☐ natural
- ☐ square
- ☐ entirely
- ☐ bamboo
- ☐ local
- ☐ rest
- ☐ to hate
- ☐ used to

dyslexic　読字障害

An Inconvenient Truth
『不都合な真実』（2006 年公開の米国ドキュメンタリー映画）

- ☐ global warming
- ☐ way
- ☐ human being
- ☐ to cause

Green School の教室内の様子。

❸ John and Cynthia wanted children to learn to live in harmony with nature. That is the reason it is called Green School. Of course, the students learn reading, writing, and arithmetic, but they also learn how to plant rice and how to cook it. They learn handcrafts like how to make a mat out of palm leaves. And they have lots of fun! They love mud wrestling in the wet rice fields, for example. The school is full of smiling faces.

❹ **The school has pre-kindergarten, kindergarten, and all 12 grades.** It also has short stay and family programs. For kids aged 14 to 17, there is a one-week Green Super Camp where the participants learn to be entrepreneurial and live a sustainable life at the same time.

- ☐ reason
- ☐ arithmetic
- ☐ to plant
- ☐ handcraft
- ☐ mat
- palm leaves ヤシの葉
- ☐ mud wrestling
- ☐ wet
- ☐ rice field
- ☐ full of
- ☐ kindergarten
- ☐ grade
- ☐ aged
- ☐ participant
- entrepreneurial 起業家の
- ☐ at the same time

Paragraph Reading

A. 第❶段落の太字の文の内容として、正しいものを選びましょう。

a. 壁がないため、グリーンスクールは学校ではない。

b. グリーンスクールは普通の学校とは違って教室に壁がない。

c. グリーンスクールは野外教室である。

B. 第❷段落の太字の文の内容として、正しいものを選びましょう。

a. グリーンスクールの創始者ジョン・ハーディは 2007 年にシンシアと結婚した。

b. ジョンとシンシアのハーディ夫妻は 2007 年にグリーンスクールを設立した。

c. ジョン・ハーディは 2007 年にグリーンスクールで妻のシンシアに初めて出会った。

C. 第❹段落の太字の文の内容として、正しいものを選びましょう。

a. グリーンスクールの学年構成は多岐にわたっている。

b. グリーンスクールの運営は 12 の団体が行っている。

c. グリーンスクールはこれから、プレ幼稚園、幼稚園などを増設する予定だ。

SECOND READING

Close Reading 形容詞と形容詞句

次の下線部の意味を a、b から選びなさい。

1. 20% of the students are <u>local Balinese children</u>.

a. 地元のバリの子どもたち

b. バリの子どもたちの地元

2. <u>The rest of the 160 students</u> come from 25 countries around the world.

a. 160 人の生徒の中の残りの生徒（160 人より少ない）

b. 残っている 160 人の生徒（160 人いる）

POINT!

名詞を詳しく説明するときには、［形容詞＋名詞］と［名詞＋前置詞＋名詞］の用法があります。日本語に訳すとき、［形容詞＋名詞］は語順どおりですが、［名詞＋前置詞＋名詞］は、後ろから訳すので注意が必要です。

1. 形容詞＋名詞	2. 名詞＋前置詞＋名詞
morning sunlight（朝の日射し）	sunlight in the morning（朝の日射し）
Spanish people（スペインの人々）	people from Spain（スペインの人々）
true moment（真実の瞬間）	moment of truth（正念場、決定的瞬間）
honorable man（尊敬すべき人）	man of honor（尊敬すべき人）

実際の文では、1 と 2 を混合した形もよく見られます。例えば、上の設問 1 の local Balinese children は <u>local</u> children <u>in Bali</u> と表現することもできます。

Reading Comprehension

本文の内容に合う文はT、合わないものはFを選びましょう。

1. グリーンスクールは人々に開かれており、風通しが良い。　[T / F]

2. ジョン・ハーディは地球温暖化の映画に感銘を受けた。　[T / F]

3. グリーンスクールはフィンランドにある。　[T / F]

Listening

DL 06　CD 1-06

①～③の音声を聞き、それぞれの内容と合うものをa、bから選びましょう。

① **a.** ジョン・ハーディーと妻のシンシアは、子どもたちが学ぶ姿を見て楽しみたかった。
　b. ジョン・ハーディーと妻のシンシアは、子どもたちに学ぶことを楽しんでもらいたかった。

② **a.** 生徒たちはハンドクラフトを習い、例えば、ヤシの葉からマットを作る。
　b. 生徒たちはハンドクラフトの授業で、ヤシの葉からマットを作るのが大好きだ。

③ **a.** 学校は満席で、経営者はニコニコしている。
　b. 学校は笑顔であふれている。

① [　　] ② [　　] ③ [　　]

REFLECTION

Fill in the Blanks

DL 07　CD 1-07

1～3の英文を聞き、空欄に語句を入れ文を完成させましょう。

1. John himself had (　　　　) (　　) (　　) to school.

2. He (　　　　) (　　) (　　　　) every day.

3. The students learn reading, writing and arithmetic, but they also learn (　　　　) (　　) (　　　　) rice and how to cook it.

Writing & Speaking

A. グリーンスクールと日本の学校の違いを箇条書きにした表を参考に、両者を比較する①〜③の文を例にならってつくってみましょう。

	Green School	Japanese school
(例)	have no walls.（壁がない）	have walls.（壁がある）
①	are open to the outdoors. （屋外に開かれている）	are not open to the outdoors. （屋外に開かれていない）
②	have natural sunlight. （自然光を使っている）	have electric lights. （電灯を使っている）
③	are made of bamboo. （竹でできている）	are made of concrete. （コンクリートでできている）

(例) The classrooms in Green School *have no walls*, but those of Japanese schools *have walls*.

① The classrooms in Green School ______________________________,

____.

② The classrooms in Green School ______________________________,

____.

③ The classrooms in Green School ______________________________,

____.

B. ペアを組み、①〜③について A さんは日本語を言い、B さんはそれに相当する英語を言いましょう。終わったら役割を交代して練習しましょう。

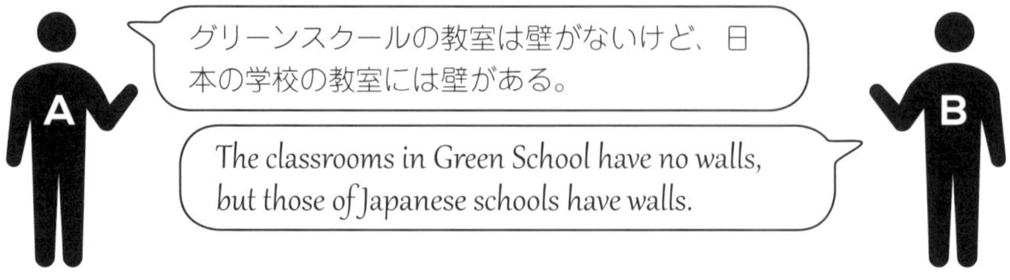

Unit 2 From Tibet with Love: *Water Rights on the Asian Continent*

LET'S START!

Guess What?

"From Tibet with Love: *Water Rights on the Asian Continent*" というタイトルから何に関する文章を予想しますか。

a. チベットのアジア人登山愛好家について

b. アジアにおけるチベットの人権問題について

c. チベット源流の河川の水を使う権利について

Check Words

A. 下線部の単語または語句の品詞に注意して、その意味をa～cから選びましょう。

1. The Mekong River's water <u>is shared</u> by Myanmar, Laos, Thailand, Cambodia, and finally Vietnam.

a. 共有されている　**b.** 分割されている　**c.** 流れている

2. The lives of millions of people <u>depend on</u> the Mekong.

a. ～の流域の　**b.** ～に左右される　**c.** ～を守っている

3. Who has the <u>right</u> to this water?

a. 右側　**b.** 正しい　**c.** 権利

4. Although dams are supposed to be a good source of renewable energy, critics say they do more <u>harm</u> than good.

a. 調和のとれた　**b.** 害　**c.** ひどく

5. These dams will greatly reduce the flow of water to <u>downstream</u> countries.

a. 下流の　**b.** 下へ押し流す　**c.** 河口

B. 上の5つの文は本文に登場するものです。これらの意味から考えて、**Guess What?** で立てた予想は正しいですか。間違っていれば、選び直しましょう。

FIRST READING

DL 08~11 CD 1-08 ~ CD 1-11

英文を読み、あとに続く問題に答えなさい。

❶ **The Mekong is one of the most important rivers of Asia.** Created from the melting snow and ice of Tibet, it flows first through China's Yunnan Province. Then as it flows southward towards the South China Sea, its water is shared by Myanmar, Laos, Thailand, Cambodia, and finally Vietnam. The lives of millions of people depend on the Mekong. It gives them water for drinking and irrigation. It also is an ecosystem that provides fish and other sources of nutrition. Who has the right to this water? **Should the people who live upstream consider the needs of the people downstream?**

❷ **This has become an urgent question as more and more water is being diverted upstream for local needs and more and more hydropower dams are being constructed along the river.** Although dams are supposed to be a good source of renewable energy, critics say they do more harm than good. Because fish cannot migrate upstream and nutritious sediment earth cannot flow downstream to fertilize the soil, they do a huge amount of ecological damage. This contributes to poverty and malnutrition among the local people. Advocates of dams say that they provide new jobs. On the other hand, critics say that traditional jobs are destroyed, and that widens the gap between rich and poor.

●●英文を読む前に●●

1. 知っている単語に☑を入れる
2. 【半数以上知っている】→英文を読み、知らない単語の意味を類推する
【半数以上わからない】→単語の意味を辞書で調べてから英文を読む

- ☐ important
- ☐ to create
- ☐ to melt
- Yunnan Province 雲南省
- ☐ to flow
- ☐ southward
- the South China Sea 南シナ海
- ☐ millions of ~
- irrigation 灌漑
- ☐ ecosystem
- ☐ to provide
- ☐ nutrition
- ☐ upstream
- ☐ to consider
- ☐ urgent
- ☐ to divert
- a hydropower dam 水力発電ダム
- ☐ to construct
- ☐ supposed to do
- ☐ renewable
- ☐ critics
- ☐ to migrate
- sediment 堆積物
- ☐ to fertilize
- ☐ soil
- ☐ huge
- ☐ amount of
- ☐ ecological
- ☐ damage
- ☐ to contribute to ~
- ☐ poverty
- ☐ malnutrition
- ☐ advocate

❸ China plans on having 28 dams along the upper Mekong River. These will greatly reduce the flow of water to downstream countries. It is also financing numerous dams in Laos and Cambodia. Laos will have some 40 dams all together. Will the people living downstream in Thailand and Vietnam have enough water in the future?

❹ All the major rivers of the Asian continent flow from Tibet. With global warming, the glaciers that feed these rivers are rapidly melting. One day Tibet will have very little water to give. **Then who will have the right to that precious water?**

- ☐ traditional
- ☐ to destroy
- ☐ to widen
- ☐ gap
- ☐ upper
- ☐ to reduce
- ☐ to finance
- ☐ numerous
- ☐ continent
- ☐ global warming
- ☐ glacier
- ☐ to feed
- ☐ rapidly
- ☐ precious

Paragraph Reading

A. 第❶段落の太字の２つの文の内容として、正しいものを選びましょう。

a. メコン川の下流の人は水を得るために上流に移住する必要がある。

b. メコン川の上流の人は下流の人も水が必要だという点を考慮すべきだ。

c. メコン川の上流の人は下流の人のことを考える必要はない。

B. 第❷段落の太字の文の内容として、正しいものを選びましょう。

a. 上流で川から水を引いたりダムを作ったりしたせいで、下流では問題が起きている。

b. 上流で川から水を引いたりダムを作ったりしたが、下流ではささいな問題だ。

c. 上流で川から水を引いたりダムを作ったりしたおかげで、下流の抱える問題が解決した。

C. 第❹段落の太字の疑問文に対する筆者の答えとしてふさわしいものを選びましょう。

a. 国内を流れる河川の水の使用権はその国にある。

b. 河川の水の使用権は流域のすべての国にある。

c. 河川の水の使用権は国際紛争に発展しやすいので、国連が持つべきだ。

SECOND READING

Close Reading 一般動詞の現在形と現在進行形

英文の（　　）に入る語句として正しいものを a ～ c から選びましょう。

1. Created from the melting snow and ice of Tibet, the Mekong (　) first through China's Yunnan Province.

a. flow　**b.** flows　**c.** flowed

2. China plans on having 28 dams and some of them (　) in China along the upper Mekong River.

a. construct　**b.** are constructing　**c.** are being constructed

POINT!

現在形	「現在の習慣」や「永遠不変の法則」など永続的な動作を表す

My father reads a newspaper every morning.
（父は毎朝、新聞を読みます）→現在の習慣

The Mekong River flows from Tibet.
（メコン川はチベットから流れています）→永遠不変の法則

※主語が 1 ～ 2 人称 (I / you) や複数の場合は動詞の原形、3 人称単数の場合は動詞に s (-es) を付ける

現在進行形 = be 動詞＋ -ing	「今している」一時的な動きや「近い将来にする・起きること」予定や予測を表す

After the rain last night, the river is flowing more rapidly than usual.
（昨夜の雨のあと、川の流れはいつもより速くなっています）→一時的な動き

They are getting married this Friday.
（彼らは今週の金曜に結婚する予定です）→近い将来に起きること

Reading Comprehension

本文の内容に合う文はT、合わないものはFを選びましょう。

1. メコン川の水を複数の国が利用している。 [T / F]

2. ダムを造っても生態系に与える影響はほとんどない。 [T / F]

3. ダムは新たな雇用を生み出す一方で、従来の仕事を奪う可能性もある。 [T / F]

Listening

DL 12 CD 1-12

①〜③の音声を聞き、それぞれの内容と合うものをa、bから選びましょう。

① **a.** 魚とそのほかの栄養源を与えてくれるのもまた経済だ。
b. 魚とそのほかの栄養源を与えてくれるのもまた生態系だ。

② **a.** 魚が下流へ移動していくと、ダムが生態系に与えるダメージは大きくなる。
b. 魚が上流へ移動できなくなるので、ダムが生態系に与えるダメージは大きい。

③ **a.** 仕事の伝統が守れられると、貧富の格差が広がると批判する人がいる。
b. 伝統的な仕事が失われ、貧富の格差が広がると批判する人がいる。

① [ ] ② [ ] ③ [ ]

REFLECTION

Fill in the Blanks

DL 13 CD 1-13

1〜3の英文を聞き、空欄に語句を入れ文を完成させましょう。

1. Then as it flows southward towards the South China Sea, its water ( ) ( ) ( ) Myanmar, Laos, Thailand, Cambodia, and finally Vietnam.

2. This ( ) ( ) ( ) and malnutrition among the local people to fertilize agricultural soil.

3. Will the people ( ) ( ) ( ) Thailand and Vietnam have enough water in the future?

Writing & Speaking

A. 本文の第❷段落では、メコン川のダム建設支持派（advocates）と懐疑派（critics）の意見が紹介されています。例にならって、日本語に合うように、その意見①、②を本文から抜き出してみましょう。

	advocates	critics
（例）	Dams are supposed to be a good source of renewable energy. （再生可能エネルギー源になる）	Dams do a huge amount of ecological damage. （生態系に甚大なダメージを与える）
	① Dams ______________________ ______________________. （新たな仕事を提供する）	② ______________________ are destroyed, and that widens ______________________. （昔ながらの仕事が失われ、貧富の格差が増大する）

B. 対立する意見をつなぐときは「逆接」の接続詞 although（～だけれども）や on the other hand（一方で）を使います。例にならって、①と②の文を although / on the other hand でつなげてみましょう。

（例） Although dams are supposed to be a good source of renewable energy, they (= dams) do a huge amount of ecological damage.
（ダムは再生可能エネルギー源となるが、生態系に甚大なダメージを与える）

Dams are supposed to be a good source of renewable energy. On the other hand, they(=dams) do a huge amount of ecological damage.
（ダムは再生可能エネルギー源となる。一方、生態系に甚大なダメージを与える）

① Although ______________________, ______________________ are destroyed, and that widens ______________________.

② ______________________. On the other hand, ______________________ are destroyed, and that widens ______________________.

C. ペアを組み、例文と①、②についてAさんは日本語を言い、Bさんはそれに相当する英語を言いましょう。終わったら役割を交代して練習しましょう。

Unit 3 How to Measure the Size of the Earth: *Simple Is Best*

LET'S START!

Guess What?

"How to Measure the Size of the Earth: *Simple Is Best*" というタイトルから何に関する文章を予想しますか。

a. 地球の大きさについて

b. 地球の大きさの測り方について

c. 質素倹約な生活について

Check Words

A. 下線部の単語または語句の品詞に注意して、その意味をａ～ｃから選びましょう。

1. In 240 BC, Eratosthenes was able to calculate the size of the Earth.
a. 計算機　**b.** 計算する　**c.** 計算上の

2. The Greeks were the first people to analyze theories.
a. 理論　**b.** 理論化する　**c.** 理論上の

3. In Syene there was a well where at noon on the day of the summer solstice, the Sun shone directly into its bottom.　**a.** 直角　**b.** 率直な　**c.** まっすぐに

4. On June 21 he put a stick into the earth at Alexandria and measured the angle between the stick's shadow and the stick.　**a.** 角度　**b.** 鋭角の　**c.** 角度をつけて

5. The distance between Alexandria and Syene was a ratio of 7.2 : 360, or 1/50 of the Earth's circumference.　**a.** 比率　**b.** 対照的な　**c.** 比較すると

B. 上の５つの文は本文に登場するものです。これらの意味から考えて、**Guess What?** で立てた予想は正しいですか。間違っていれば、選び直しましょう。

FIRST READING

DL 14~17　CD 1-14 ~ CD 1-17

英文を読み、あとに続く問題に答えなさい。

❶ **In 240 BC, a Greek man called Eratosthenes was able to calculate the size of the Earth.** How in the world did he do it? He had no calculator, and, of course, no computer. **He used only a stick and his ability to analyze.**

❷ Science started with the Greeks. Because people were allowed to think freely, they could develop new ideas and then question if those ideas were correct. They were the first people to analyze theories. You know the famous mathematical theorem $a^2+b^2=c^2$. It was discovered in the 6th century BC by Pythagoras.

❸ **Eratosthenes worked in Egypt at the famous Library of Alexandria, which was the most respected institution of learning in the world at the time.** There he heard about a well where at noon on June 21 each year, the day of the summer solstice, the Sun shone directly into the bottom of the well. This gave Eratosthenes a plan for measuring the size of the Earth. The well was in Syene, 800 km away from Alexandria. So, on June 21 he stood a stick into the earth at Alexandria. Then he measured the angle that was made between the top of the stick and its shadow. It was 7.2°. The Greeks knew that the world was round, so Eratosthenes calculated that the distance between Alexandria and Syene was a ratio of 7.2 : 360, or 1/50 of the

●●英文を読む前に●●

1. 知っている単語に ☑ を入れる
2. 【半数以上知っている】
→英文を読み、知らない単語の意味を類推する
【半数以上わからない】
→単語の意味を辞書で調べてから英文を読む

☐ Greek

Eratosthenes エラトステネス（古代ギリシャの数学者）

☐ calculator

☐ stick

☐ ability

☐ to analyze

☐ to allow

☐ freely

☐ to develop

☐ correct

☐ mathematical

☐ theorem

☐ to discover

Pythagoras ピタゴラス（古代ギリシャの数学者）

☐ respected

☐ institution

☐ at the time

☐ well

summer solstice 夏至

☐ bottom

☐ to measure

Syene シエネ（現在のエジプト南部アスワンにあたる）

☐ away from ~

Alexandria アレクサンドリア（紀元前 332 年に、アレクサンダー大王により建設。現在はエジプト第 2 の都市）

☐ to stand

☐ shadow

☐ round

☐ distance

Earth's circumference. The rest of the equation was easy. The distance between the two towns (800 km) × 50 = 39,000 km. That is an error of less than 2%!

❹ Eratosthenes also calculated the size of the Moon, as well as its distance from the Earth. He did this by comparing the size of the Earth's shadow on the Moon during a lunar eclipse. **His discoveries show that analysis is a wonderful tool that anyone can use—and the best part is that it's free!**

circumference 外周
- □ rest
- □ equation
- □ error
- □ less than ~
- □ A as well as B
- □ to compare

lunar eclipse 月食
- □ discovery
- □ analysis
- □ wonderful
- □ tool

Paragraph Reading

A. 第❶段落の太字の 2 つの文の内容として、正しいものを選びましょう。

a. このエッセーは、エラトステネスの人生について書いている。

b. このエッセーは、紀元前 240 年当時の地球の様子について紹介している。

c. このエッセーは、ギリシャ人による地球の大きさの計測方法を説明している。

B. 第❸段落の太字の文の内容として、正しいものを選びましょう。

a. エラトステネスは当時の世界で有数の研究機関で働いていた。

b. エラトステネスのおかげでアレクサンドリアの図書館は世界一になった。

c. 当時、エラトステネスはエジプトでもっとも尊敬されていた。

C. 第❹段落の太字の文の内容として、正しいものを選びましょう。

a. 地道に都市と都市の距離を測ることは誰にもできる確実な方法だ。

b. 論理的思考はお金もかからず誰にでもできる。

c. エラトステネスは、誰にでも簡単に使いこなせる計算機を作った。

SECOND READING

Close Reading 動詞の過去形

次の英文の（　　）内の動詞を過去形にして文を完成させましょう。

1. The well (is) in Syene, 800 km away from Alexandria. ________

2. Eratosthenes (have) no calculator. ________

3. The Greeks (know) that the world was round. ________

4. This (give) Eratosthenes a plan for measuring the size of the Earth. ________

5. They (are) the first people to analyze theories. ________

POINT!

動詞の過去形は、歴史的事実など過去に起きた出来事を時系列に説明するときに使います。「昔はそうだったけれど、今はそうではない」という意味合いを含む場合もあります。
一般動詞を過去形にする方法には、語尾に -ed(d) をつけるだけの規則活用のほかに、不規則活用があります（不規則活用については巻末の不規則動詞活用表も参照）。be 動詞の場合、is / am の過去形は was、are の過去形は were になります。

[規則活用]

Pythagoras **discovered** the famous mathematical theorem $a^2+b^2=c^2$ in the 6th century BC.
（紀元前 6 世紀にピタゴラスは三平方の定理を発見した）→歴史的事実

[不規則活用]

On June 21, he **stood** a stick into the earth at Alexandria and measured the angle that was **made** between the top of the stick and its shadow.
（6 月 21 日にアレクサンドリアで地面に棒を立て、できた影と棒の先端同士の角度を測った）

Reading Comprehension

本文の内容に合う文はT、合わないものはFを選びましょう。

1. 古代ギリシャでは自由な発想ができたので、ものごとに疑問を抱く人はいなかった。 [T / F]

2. 夏至の日の正午、エラトステネスはアレクサンドリアで地面に棒を垂直に立て、棒の先端と影の先端の角度を測った。 [T / F]

3. アレクサンドリアとシエナの距離は800 kmで、地球の外周の比率は7.2：360であることから、エラトステネスは地球の外周を計算した。 [T / F]

Listening

DL 18　CD 1-18

①～③の音声を聞き、それぞれの内容と合うものをa、bから選びましょう。

① **a.** 世界でエラトステネス以外に誰が地球の大きさを計算したのか。
　b. 一体全体どうやってエラトステネスは地球の大きさを計算したのか。

② **a.** 自由に考えることを許されていたので、新しい考えを発展することができた。
　b. 考えるだけならばお金がかからないので、新しい考えを発展することができた。

③ **a.** エラトステネスは計算せずにアレクサンドリアとシエナの距離を割り出した。
　b. エラトステネスは計算してアレクサンドリアとシエナの距離の比率を出した。

① [　　] ② [　　] ③ [　　]

REFLECTION

Fill in the Blanks

DL 19　CD 1-19

1～3の英文を聞き、空欄に語句を入れ文を完成させましょう。

1. They were (　　) (　　　　) (　　　　) to analyze theories.

2. They could develop new ideas and (　　　　) (　　　　　　) (　　) those ideas were correct.

3. That is an error (　　) (　　　　) (　　　　) 2%!

Writing & Speaking

A. 過去の出来事を時系列に語るとき、「はじめに」「それから」「最後に」といったつなぎ語を文頭につけると、前後関係がわかりやすくなります。 のつなぎ語が表の3つのどれに分類されるかを考え、空欄に書き込んでみましょう。

はじめに	それから	最後に

afterwards / finally / then / in the end / at first / firstly / lastly / at the beginning / after that

B. 日本語を参考に上のつなぎ語を空欄に入れて、野口英世の生涯を説明する英文を完成させましょう。

① 野口英世は 1876 年に福島県で生まれた。1 歳半の時、左手に大やけどを負う。＿その後＿、左手で物を握れなくなる。	Hideyo Noguchi was born in 1876. When he was one and a half years old, his left hand was severely burnt. ＿＿＿＿＿, he was unable to hold anything with his left hand.
② 15 歳の時、友人の寄付で手術を受け、＿それから＿、左手を使えるようになる。	At the age of 15, his friends donated money for an operation. ＿＿＿＿＿, he could use his left hand.
③ 20 歳で医者になり、＿はじめに＿細菌学を研究した。	He became a doctor at the age of 20. ＿＿＿＿＿, he studied bacteriology.
④ ＿次に＿アメリカで蛇の毒を研究し、＿最後に＿アフリカで黄熱病の研究中に亡くなった。	＿＿＿＿＿, he studied snake poison in the United States. ＿＿＿＿＿, he died in Africa while he was studying yellow fever.

C. ペアを組み、完成した英文を比較してみましょう。最後に①〜④についてAさんは日本語を言い、Bさんはそれに相当する英語を言いましょう。終わったら役割を交代して練習しましょう。

Unit 4 Being Green: *The Example of a Famous Hotel*

LET'S START!

Guess What?

"Being Green: *The Example of a Famous Hotel*" というタイトルから何に関する文章を予想しますか。

a. 緑色をトレードマークにした有名ホテル

b. 植物に囲まれたホテル

c. 環境に優しいことを意識したホテル

Check Words

A. 下線部の単語または語句の品詞に注意して、その意味を a ～ c から選びましょう。

1. Green is the new culture. **a.** 環境に優しいこと **b.** 緑色の **c.** 植物の

2. It is difficult for a hotel to be environmentally conscious without annoying the guests.
a. 良い環境 **b.** 環境に配慮している **c.** 環境問題を引き起こす

3. One strategy is educating guests to support the environment through everyday actions, donations, and volunteerism.
a. 教えること **b.** 学習中の **c.** 教育にたずさわる

4. The impact a person leaves on the environment is called the environmental footprint. **a.** 踏みつける **b.** 印刷 **c.** 足跡

5. The water you use, the food you eat, the clothes you wear, the train you ride—all leave an impact. **a.** 影響 **b.** 効果的に **c.** 衝撃的な

B. 上の 5 つの文は本文に登場するものです。これらの意味から考えて、**Guess What?** で立てた予想は正しいですか。間違っていれば、選び直しましょう。

FIRST READING

DL 20~23　CD 1-20 ~ CD 1-23

英文を読み、あとに続く問題に答えなさい。

❶ **From electric cars to biodegradable shopping bags, being "green" and "organic" is on the mind of producers and consumers alike.** Wherever you go in the United States, you will find products that advertise how green they are, for instance, using vegetable-based ink for printing or paper made from a fast growing grass called kenaf instead of wood. Green is the new culture.

❷ **Hotels, too, have tried to be green by turning up the temperature in the guest rooms in summer or asking the guests to use the bed sheets twice.** Yet it is difficult for a hotel to be environmentally conscious without annoying the guests. Marriott International is proving it can. One of the top hotel chains in the world, Marriott has committed to an energy-saving program at 264 of its hotels in the United States. Marriott saves on electricity bills and also earns incentive payments from utility companies as a reward for reducing use during peak periods of demand. The financial reward is not the prime motive, however. It is the ethics.

❸ Reducing the environmental impact of its business is seen as corporate responsibility. Among the strategies listed on the Marriott website are the following:

1. Reducing waste and the consumption of water.

●●英文を読む前に●●

1. 知っている単語に☑を入れる
2. 【半数以上知っている】→英文を読み、知らない単語の意味を類推する
【半数以上わからない】→単語の意味を辞書で調べてから英文を読む

単語リスト／語注

- □ electric
- biodegradable 生分解できる
- □ organic
- □ on the mind of ~
- □ producer
- □ consumer
- □ alike
- □ wherever
- □ to advertise
- □ for instance
- □ vegetable-based
- □ made from ~
- □ fast
- □ grass
- kenaf ケナフ（西アフリカ原産の植物）
- □ instead of
- □ to turn up
- □ temperature
- □ twice
- □ to annoy
- □ to prove
- □ to commit
- □ energy-saving
- □ electricity bill
- □ to earn
- □ incentive payment
- □ utility company
- □ reward
- □ to reduce
- □ peak

2. Using environmentally-friendly materials, including shower heads that use less water, light bulbs that use 80% less energy, and key cards made of recycled materials.
3. Educating guests to support the environment through everyday actions, donations, and volunteerism.

❹ The impact a person leaves on the environment is called an environmental footprint. It is impossible as a human being not to leave an impact. The water you use, the food you eat, the clothes you wear, the train you ride—all leave an impact. **However, like the Marriott, we can make an effort to leave as small a footprint as possible.**

- ☐ financial
- ☐ prime
- ☐ motive
- ☐ ethic
- ☐ corporate responsibility
- ☐ strategy
- ☐ waste
- ☐ consumption
- ☐ material
- ☐ to include
- ☐ a light bulb
- ☐ made of ~
- ☐ recycled
- ☐ to support
- ☐ a donation
- ☐ volunteerism
- ☐ impossible
- ☐ to make an effort
- ☐ as ~ as possible

Paragraph Reading

A. 第❶段落の太字の文の内容として、正しいものを選びましょう。

a. 電気自動車や買い物袋はオーガニックを前面に出した方がよく売れる。

b. 様々な製品に、環境への意識が反映されている。

c. 人々は電気自動車や買い物袋から自然を感じ取る。

B. 第❷段落の太字の文の内容として、正しいものを選びましょう。

a. ホテルも部屋の設定温度を上げるなど、環境に配慮した取り組みをしている。

b. ベッドメイキングを二回行うホテルが人気である。

c. 植物を置いて涼しげな環境を演出するホテルが増えた。

C. 第❹段落の太字の文の内容として、正しいものを選びましょう。

a. マリオットホテルのように、足跡を減らすことが重要である。

b. マリオットホテルは環境に配慮した素晴らしいホテルである。

c. われわれは環境への負荷をできるだけ減らす努力ができる。

SECOND READING

Close Reading 動名詞

英文の下線部の意味を a、b から選びましょう。

1. Yet it is difficult for a hotel to be environmentally conscious <u>without annoying the guests</u>.

a. 客を困らせて **b.** 客を困らせることなく

2. <u>Reducing the environmental impact of its business</u> is seen as corporate responsibility.

a. 企業活動が環境に与える影響を減らすこと

b. 企業活動が環境に与える影響を減らしている

POINT!

語形	動詞の原形 +ing
意味	「～すること」

動詞的性質	**名詞的性質**
動詞のように目的語や補語を取る	名詞のように主語や目的語や補語になる
He remembered <u>**drinking**</u> coffee. （彼はコーヒーを飲んだことを覚えていました）	My hobby is <u>**jogging**</u>. （趣味はジョギングです）
I am sick of <u>**being**</u> a taxi driver. （タクシーの運転手の仕事はもううんざりです）	<u>**Jogging**</u> is fun for me. （ジョギングすることは楽しいです）

動名詞を目的語に取る動詞には、admit, avoid, dislike, enjoy, finish, recall, stop などがある。ただし、begin, continue, forget, hate, like, love, prefer, regret, remember, start, try といった動詞は、動名詞も不定詞も両方取ることができる。

Reading Comprehension

本文の内容に合う文はT、合わないものはFを選びましょう。

1. マリオットホテルはアメリカ国内の同ホテルでエネルギー節約プログラムを実施している。 [T / F]

2. マリオットホテルの顧客は環境に関する講義を受ける。 [T / F]

3. 人が環境に与える負荷は、環境フットプリントと呼ばれる。 [T / F]

Listening

DL 24 CD 1-24

①～③の音声を聞き、それぞれの内容と合うものをa、bから選びましょう。

① **a.** アメリカのどこに行っても、環境への取り組みを宣伝した製品を目にする。
b. アメリカであなたが行く場所には、緑色の製品が多い。

② **a.** 水、食べ物、服、電車が環境フットプリントにとって重要である。
b. 水、食べ物、服、電車など、これらすべてが環境フットプリントを残す。

③ **a.** 寄付やボランティアなどを通じて、環境をサポートするように宿泊客を教育すること。
b. 毎日の行動を宿泊客に見せることによって、環境をサポートする姿勢をアピールすること。

① [ ] ② [ ] ③ [ ]

REFLECTION

Fill in the Blanks

DL 25 CD 1-25

1～3の英文を聞き、空欄に語句を入れ文を完成させましょう。

1. Hotels have tried to ( ) green by ( ) ( ) the ( ) in the guest rooms in summer.

2. It is difficult ( ) be ( ) conscious ( ) annoying the guests.

3. Marriott ( ) incentive payments from utility companies as a ( ) for ( ) use during peak periods.

Writing & Speaking

A. 本文で使われた「できるかぎり～」を意味する as ~ as possible の表現を用いて、マリオットホテル内で環境のためにされている①～③のことを英語で書いてましょう。

	誰が	何をどうする	どのように
(例)	You	(何回も練習する)	as many ~ as possible
①	Hotels	(水を使う)	as little ~ as possible
②	Guests	(タオルを使う)	as few ~ as possible
③	Hotels	(ごみを減らす)	as much ~ as possible

(例) You should *practice* as many *times* as possible.
(あなたはできるだけ何回も練習すべきです)

① Hotels should ______________________________
______________________________.

② Guests should ______________________________
______________________________.

③ Hotels should ______________________________
______________________________.

B. ペアを組み、①～③について A さんが日本語を言ったら、B さんはそれに相当する英語で返しましょう。終わったら役割を交代して練習しましょう。

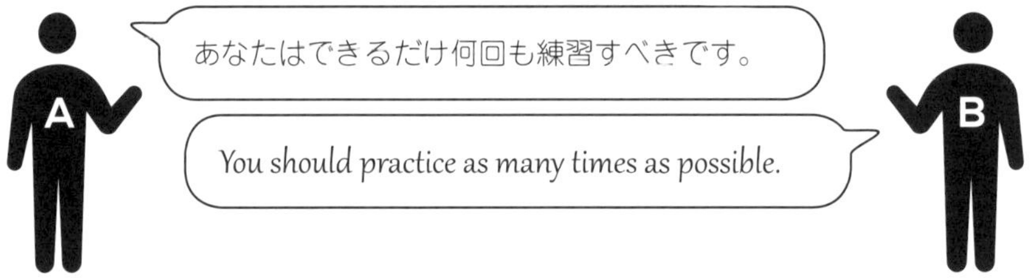

Unit 5 How to Live to Be 100: *Three Examples*

LET'S START!

Guess What?

"How to Live to Be 100: *Three Examples*" というタイトルから何に関する文章を予想しますか。

a. 100 通りの人生

b. 100%満足する生き方の 3 つの例

c. 100 歳まで生きる秘訣

Check Words

A. 下線部の単語または語句の品詞に注意して、その意味を a ～ c から選びましょう。

1. In all three places "old" people are <u>energetic</u>.
a. エネルギー　**b.** 活動的な　**c.** 活発に

2. There is a high ratio of people <u>over</u> 100.
a. ～を終える　**b.** ～を超える　**c.** ～の外の

3. The most important <u>factor</u> for their long, healthy lives was lifestyle.
a. 事実　**b.** 工場　**c.** 要因

4. In Okinawa, old women <u>have an important role</u> in religious rites.
a. 重要な機会をもつ　**b.** 重要な役割を果たす　**c.** 重要視する

5. Having a do-it-yourself <u>attitude</u> is a key to a long, happy life.
a. 姿勢　**b.** 試みる　**c.** 適切な

B. 上の 5 つの文は本文に登場するものです。これらの意味から考えて、**Guess What?** で立てた予想は正しいですか。間違っていれば、選び直しましょう。

FIRST READING

DL 26~30　CD 1-26 ~ CD 1-30

英文を読み、あとに続く問題に答えなさい。

❶ **Being young is awfully nice. Being old can be, too, especially if you are healthy and productive.** A study was made of three places in the world where there is a high ratio of people over 100. The first place the researchers visited was in the mountains of Sardinia, an island off the coast of Italy. The next was Okinawa. The third was a community of Seventh-day Adventists living near Los Angeles. In all three places "old" people are energetic and mentally active.

❷ **The researchers found that the most important factor for their long, healthy lives was the food they eat.** All of them eat mostly vegetables. The Sardinians have a diet based on homegrown fruits and vegetables such as eggplant, tomatoes, and beans. The Okinawans eat a lot of tofu, seaweed, and citrus fruit. The Adventists eat whole wheat bread, nuts, fruit, and soymilk. They eat very little meat or none at all. They don't smoke or drink, either. Although the Sardinians do, they drink a kind of red wine that may help prevent cardiovascular disease.

❸ The next important factor was having strong family bonds and many friends. Marge Jetton, who is 103, volunteers at a senior center near Los Angeles, and she drives there herself.

❹ Equally significant was being physically active. Giuseppe Cugusi at 85 still raises pigs

●●英文を読む前に●●

1. 知っている単語に ☑ を入れる
2. 【半数以上知っている】
→英文を読み、知らない単語の意味を類推する
【半数以上わからない】
→単語の意味を辞書で調べてから英文を読む

- ☐ awfully
- ☐ especially
- ☐ healthy
- ☐ productive
- ☐ ratio
- ☐ researcher
- ☐ coast
- ☐ community

Seventh-day Adventists
セブンス・デイ・アドベンチスト教徒

- ☐ mentally
- ☐ vegetable
- ☐ diet
- ☐ homegrown
- ☐ eggplant
- ☐ seaweed
- ☐ citrus fruit
- ☐ whole wheat
- ☐ soymilk
- ☐ not ~, either
- ☐ to prevent

cardiovascular　心臓血管の

- ☐ disease
- ☐ bond
- ☐ volunteer
- ☐ senior center
- ☐ equally
- ☐ significant
- ☐ physically

in Sardinia, Italy. "I've been working all my life, even when I don't feel great," he says. "If I stayed home all day, then I'd be sick."

❺ Basically, the researchers found that eating simply and healthfully, being committed to family, friends, and community, and having a do-it-yourself attitude were the keys to a long, happy life.

- ☐ to raise
- ☐ pig
- ☐ basically
- ☐ healthfully
- ☐ to commit
- ☐ do-it-yourself

Paragraph Reading

A. 第❶段落の太字の２つの文の内容として、正しいものを選びましょう。

a. 若さはあまりよいことではない。

b. 年を取ることはよくない。

c. 年をとっても健康に活動できれば素晴らしい。

B. 第❷段落の太字の文の内容として、正しいものを選びましょう。

a. 健康で長く生きるための重要な要因は食べものにあった。

b. 健康で長く生きることが人生の最も重要な目標だった。

c. 重要な調査対象は健康で長生きしている人たちだった。

C. 第❺段落の太字の文の内容として、正しいものを選びましょう。

a. 調査でわかった長寿の要因は食事、人との関わり、自分でやるという態度の３つである。

b. 調査でわかった長寿の要因は３つだけではない。

c. 今後の調査でさらに長寿の要因がわかるだろう。

SECOND READING

Close Reading　現在分詞と過去分詞

英文の下線部の意味を a、b から選びましょう。

1. The third was a community of <u>Seventh-day Adventists living near Los Angeles</u>.

a. ロサンジェルスの近くに住んでいるセブンス・デイ・アドベンチスト教徒

b. ロサンジェルスの近くにあるセブンス・デイ・アドベンチスト教徒の住居

2. The Sardinians have <u>a diet based on vegetables</u>.

a. 野菜を基礎にした食事　**b.** 食事の基礎となった野菜

3. They eat <u>homegrown fruit</u>.

a. 家で食べられている果物　**b.** 家で栽培された果物

POINT!

	形	意味
現在分詞	動詞＋ ing	～している（進行中）
過去分詞	（規則変化の場合は）動詞＋～ ed	～された（受動態）

●現在分詞と過去分詞には名詞を修飾する働きがあります。現在分詞は進行中（～が…している）、過去分詞のときは受動態（～が…された）という意味になります。

●過去分詞は規則変化の場合は過去形と同じ（like → liked）ですが、不規則に変化する動詞も数多く存在します（詳しくは巻末の不規則動詞活用表を参照）。

[The man] <u>driving the blue car</u> is my brother.
（青い車を運転している男性は私の兄だ〈男が青い車を運転している〉）

[The car] <u>parked outside the house</u> is my brother's.
（家の外に駐車されている車は兄の車だ〈車が駐車されている〉）

Reading Comprehension

本文の内容に合う文はT、合わないものはFを選びましょう。

1. サルディーニャ島はほかの調査地よりも健康な高齢者が多い。 [T / F]

2. 長寿の多い土地では肉をほとんど食べない。 [T / F]

3. 自分のことは自分でやる人は健康で長生きだ。 [T / F]

Listening

DL 31 CD 1-31

①〜③の音声を聞き、それぞれの内容と合うものをa、bから選びましょう。

① **a.** 3か所で100人を超える人が調査された。
b. 100歳以上の人の割合が高い3か所で調査が行われた。

② **a.** サルディーニャ島の人は豆など野菜中心の食事をとっている。
b. サルディーニャ島の人は野菜中心の食事だが豆は取らない。

③ **a.** 一日中家にいたら、よく休めるだろう。
b. 一日中家にいたら、病気になってしまうだろう。

① [ ] ② [ ] ③ [ ]

REFLECTION

Fill in the Blanks

DL 32 CD 1-32

1〜3の英文を聞き、空欄に語句を入れ文を完成させましょう。

1. They eat very little meat or ( ) ( ) ( ).

2. Giuseppe Cugusi ( ) ( ) ( ) raises pigs.

3. ( ) ( ) ( ) all my life, even when I don't feel great.

Writing & Speaking

A. 次に挙げるのは健康的に痩せる３つの秘訣です。①～③の日本語に相当する英語を右の A ～ C から選びましょう。

健康的に痩せる３つの秘訣	Three factors for keeping fit
①十分に運動をする	**A.** eat lots of vegetables
②野菜を十分にとる	**B.** have friends
③友人を持つ	**C.** get plenty of exercise

① [　　] ② [　　] ③ [　　]

B. 上記①～③の語句を適切な形に変えて下線に入れ、次の文章を完成させましょう。

There are three major factors for keeping fit: the most important factor is ______________________. Another factor is ______________________. Finally, ______________________ ______________________ is also a key for a long, healthy life.

C. ペアを組み、①～③についてＡさんは日本語を言い、Ｂさんはそれに相当する英語を言いましょう。終わったら役割を交代して練習しましょう。

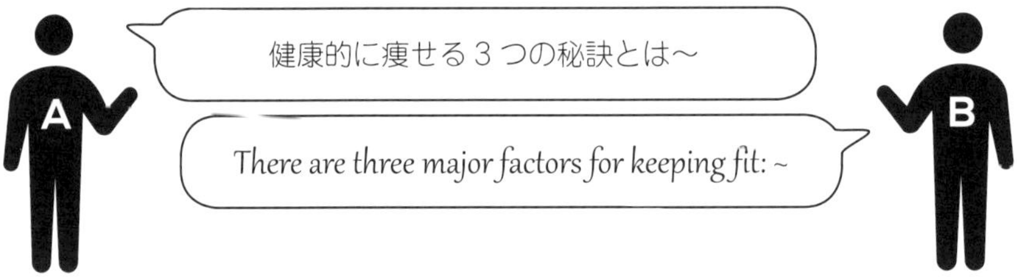

A
健康的に痩せる３つの秘訣とは～
There are three major factors for keeping fit: ~
B

Unit 6 The Great Pacific Garbage Patch: *What We Have Done to the Sea*

LET'S START!

Guess What?

"The Great Pacific Garbage Patch: *What We Have Done to the Sea*" というタイトルから何に関する文章を予想しますか。

a. 海の生き物の話

b. 太平洋の海流の話

c. 海洋ごみの話

Check Words

A. 下線部の単語または語句の品詞に注意して、その意味をa～cから選びましょう。

1. No matter what time of day I looked, there was plastic everywhere.
a. プラスチック　**b.** プラスチックのような　**c.** 平板

2. The floating debris breaks down and becomes small pieces that are suspended in the water.　**a.** 壊れた　**b.** 油　**c.** 破片

3. The plastic absorbs pollutants in the seawater.
a. 石鹸　**b.** 吸収する　**c.** 理解する

4. As for larger pieces of plastic, they end up in the stomachs of marine birds and animals.　**a.** 胃　**b.** 上司　**c.** ためこむ

5. Their stomachs are filled with bottle caps, cigarette lighters and even toothbrushes.
a. ～に満足で　**b.** ～でいっぱいで　**c.** ～と一緒に詰められて

B. 上の5つの文は本文に登場するものです。これらの意味から考えて、**Guess What?** で立てた予想は正しいですか。間違っていれば、選び直しましょう。

FIRST READING

DL 33~36 CD 1-33 ~ CD 1-36

英文を読み、あとに続く問題に答えなさい。

❶ **There is an area in the Pacific Ocean where all the trash that floats in the ocean between Japan and North America is brought together by the ocean currents.** It was discovered in 1997 by racing boat captain Charles Moore when he was sailing from Hawaii back to California. For a whole week, "no matter what time of day I looked, there was plastic everywhere," he recalls. It was "unbelievable." Twice the size of Texas, this collection of debris has been called the "Great Pacific Garbage Patch." Some of this garbage comes from ships, but most comes from land, having been thrown into rivers, washed to the sea by rain, or blown by the wind.

❷ **Not all the plastic trash is visible. Some of it sinks and covers the ocean floor where it kills the creatures at the bottom.** The floating debris breaks down and becomes small pieces that are suspended in the water. This "soup," as Moore calls it, is 100 meters deep in places. Fish then eat these particles along with the plankton. Because the plastic absorbs pollutants in the seawater, including PCBs, DDT, and PAHs, those toxins then enter the food chain. What are the consequences for humans?

❸ As for larger pieces of plastic, they end up in the stomachs of marine birds and animals.

●●英文を読む前に●●

1. 知っている単語に ☑ を入れる
2. 【半数以上知っている】
→英文を読み、知らない単語の意味を類推する
【半数以上わからない】
→単語の意味を辞書で調べてから英文を読む

- ☐ area
- ☐ the Pacific Ocean
- ☐ trash
- ☐ to float
- ☐ to bring together
- ☐ ocean current
- ☐ to discover
- ☐ whole
- ☐ to recall
- ☐ unbelievable
- ☐ twice
- ☐ garbage
- ☐ patch
- ☐ to throw
- ☐ to wash
- ☐ to blow
- ☐ visible
- ☐ to sink
- ☐ ocean floor
- ☐ creature
- ☐ bottom
- ☐ to break down
- ☐ piece
- ☐ to suspend
- ☐ particle
- ☐ plankton
- ☐ pollutant
- ☐ seawater
- ☐ toxin
- ☐ food chain
- ☐ consequence
- ☐ as for
- ☐ to end up

Sea turtles gulp down plastic bags that look like their favorite food, jellyfish. An albatross will pick up brightly colored things to feed her chick. Thousands of chicks die every year from starvation because their stomachs are filled with plastic things like bottle caps, cigarette lighters and even toothbrushes.

❹ **Plastics never disappear. They will photo-degrade into tiny microscopic particles but not biodegrade.** They become part of the whole ecosystem—the fish, the seaweed, the sand. In what way are you part of the great plastic debris?

- □ turtle
- □ to gulp down
- □ jellyfish
- □ albatross
- □ to pick up
- □ to feed
- □ chick
- □ to die from
- □ starvation
- □ to disappear
- □ toothbrush
- □ to photodegrade
- □ tiny
- □ microscopic
- □ to biodegrade
- □ ecosystem
- □ seaweed
- □ sand

Paragraph Reading

A. 第❶段落の太字の文の内容として、正しいものを選びましょう。

a. 太平洋の一部の地域に日本と北米が様々なごみを捨てている。

b. 海流によって海洋ごみが集まる区域が太平洋にある。

c. 環太平洋地域は大量のごみが捨てられる地域である。

B. 第❷段落の太字の文の内容として、正しいものを選びましょう。

a. 海底にたまったプラスチックは生き物を死なせている。

b. プラスチックごみは透明なため、生き物が誤って飲み込んでしまう。

c. 海上のプラスチックごみは見えないため、生き物がぶつかって死ぬことがある。

C. 第❹段落の太字の文の内容として、正しいものを選びましょう。

a. プラスチックごみは消えることはなく、今後も使用されるだろう。

b. あまりに量が多いため、プラスチックごみを集めることはできない。

c. プラスチックごみは粒子になるが生物によって分解されることはない。

SECOND READING

Close Reading 疑問詞

英文の下線部の意味を a、b から選びましょう。

1. What are the consequences for humans?

a. 人間にもたらされる結果は何か。

b. いつ人間に結果がもたらされるか。

2. In what way are you part of the great plastic debris?

a. 何が原因で　**b.** どんなふうに

POINT!

いつ（when）どこで（where）誰が（who）何を（what）どのように（how）ということを尋ねるときは、疑問詞を使い、次の語順で疑問文を作ります。

疑問詞	動詞	主語＋動詞ほか	意味
When	do	you leave?	**いつ**出かけますか。
Who	is	your teacher?	あなたの先生は**誰**ですか。
How	is	your mother?	あなたのお母さんは（お加減）**いかが**ですか。
Where	do	you live?	あなたは**どこに**住んでいますか。
What	are	you doing?	**何**をしているのですか。

how や what は他の語句と結びついて使うこともあります。

疑問詞	動詞	主語＋動詞ほか	意味
How often	do	you play baseball?	**どのくらい頻繁に**野球をしますか。
What color	is	your car?	あなたの車は**何色**ですか。
In what way	do	you save money?	**どのようにして**貯金していますか。
Which way	leads	to the station?	**どちらの道**が駅に通じていますか。

Reading Comprehension

本文の内容に合う文はT、合わないものはFを選びましょう。

1. テキサス州の3倍ほどの広さの海域に海洋ごみが集まっている。 [T / F]

2. プラスチックは小さな破片となって海中を漂う。 [T / F]

3. 様々な生き物がプラスチックの破片を誤飲して死んでしまう。 [T / F]

Listening

DL 37 CD 1-37

①〜③の音声を聞き、それぞれの内容と合うものをa、bから選びましょう。

① **a.** どの場所から見ても、それはプラスチックに違いなかった。
b. いつ見ても、あらゆるところにプラスチックが浮いていた。

② **a.** 海から出るごみと陸から出るごみは異なる性質をもつ。
b. 陸で出たごみも雨や風によって海まで届く。

③ **a.** 大きなプラスチック片は、海鳥や海洋生物の胃の中に堆積する。
b. 海鳥や海洋生物の胃の中で、プラスチック片が巨大化することがわかった。

① [ ] ② [ ] ③ [ ]

REFLECTION

Fill in the Blanks

DL 38 CD 1-38

1〜3の英文を聞き、空欄に語句を入れ文を完成させましょう。

1. The Great Pacific Garbage Patch was ( ) by Charles Moore when he was sailing ( ) Hawaii ( ) California.

2. Some ( ) this garbage sinks and covers the ocean floor where it kills the ( ) at the ( ).

3. Thousands of chicks die ( ) starvation because their stomachs are filled ( ) plastic things ( ) bottle caps.

Writing & Speaking

A. 次の表は (A) が「どんなに～であろうとも」という条件、(B) が「誰がどうする」という結果を表しています。

①～④の日本語に相当する英語を完成させましょう。(A) は (　　) に入る語を a ～ c から選び、(B) は [　　] 内の語を並べ替えてください。

	(A) どんなに～であろうとも	(B) 誰がどうする
①	どんなやり方を試しても No matter (　　) I try, **a.** how　**b.** way　**c.** what	私は彼の名前を発音できない。 ____________________. [can't / his / I / name / pronounce]
②	私がいつ行っても No matter (　　) I go, **a.** time　**b.** how often　**c.** when	彼はそこにいない。 ____________________. [not / he / is / there]
③	彼が何を言おうと No matter (　　) he says, **a.** how much　**b.** what　**c.** words	あなたはよくやった。 ____________________. [did / good / you / job / a]
④	彼はどこに行こうとも No matter (　　) he goes, **a.** places　**b.** where　**c.** which	彼はすぐ友達ができる。 ____________________. [he / friends soon / makes]

B. ペアを組み、①～④について A さんが日本語を言ったら、B さんはそれに相当する英語で返しましょう。終わったら役割を交代して練習しましょう。

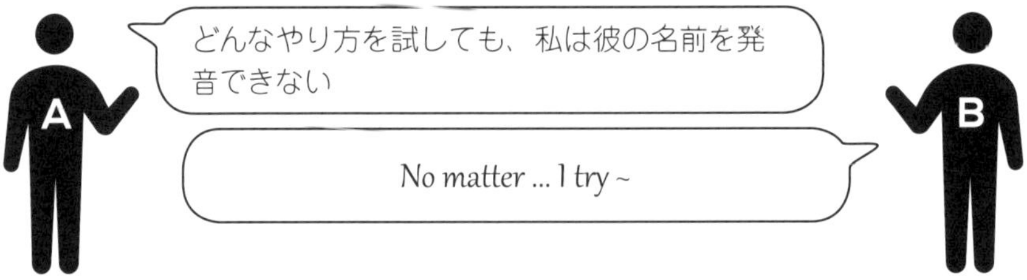

Unit 7

Free Solo Climbing: *Doing What's Impossible*

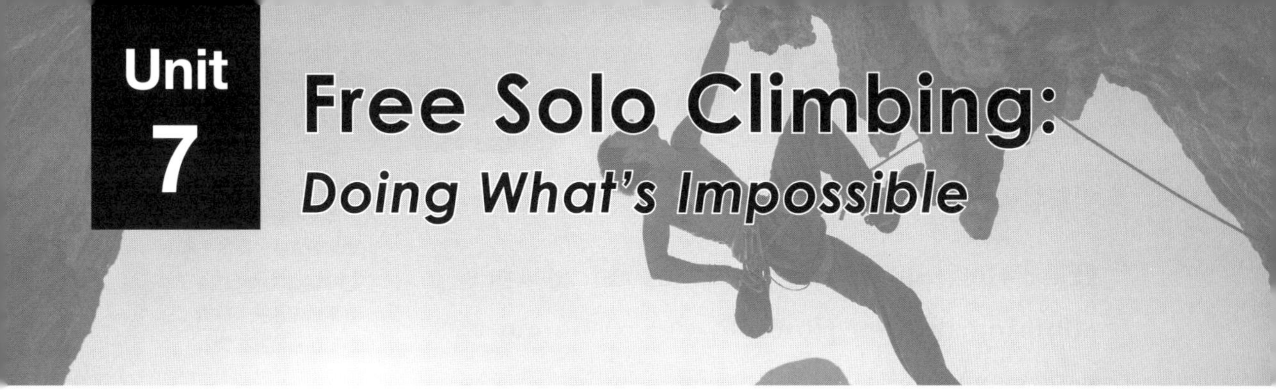

LET'S START!

Guess What?

"Free Solo Climbing: *Doing What's Impossible*" というタイトルから何に関する文章を予想しますか。

a. 一人でフリークライミングをするのは不可能だ

b. 一人でフリークライミングという不可能なことにトライする

c. 不可能なことを除外して可能な範囲でフリークライミングをする

Check Words

A. 下線部の単語または語句の品詞に注意して、その意味をa～cから選びましょう。

1. A solo free climber has nothing but his climbing shoes.

a. ～以外は何も持たない　**b.** ～すらない　**c.** ～を物ともしない

2. If he makes a mistake, he will die.

a. 大金を稼ぐ　**b.** 進む　**c.** 間違う

3. Yosemite has walls that are absolutely steep.

a. 急こう配の　**b.** 巨大な　**c.** そびえ立つ

4. His famous climbs were all done "on sight".

a. 見える範囲で　**b.** 光景の中で　**c.** その場で

5. Valuing a "genuine experience," he doesn't think highly of today's climbers who research the route.

a. ～の高さを測る　**b.** ～を高く評価する　**c.** ～を高価だと思う

B. 上の5つの文は本文に登場するものです。これらの意味から考えて、**Guess What?** で立てた予想は正しいですか。間違っていれば、選び直しましょう。

FIRST READING

DL 39~42　CD 1-39 ~ CD 1-42

英文を読み、あとに続く問題に答えなさい。

❶ **At the top of the risky world of rock climbing is Alex Honnold.** Agile and quick, he does what is called "free solo climbing." It is the ultimate in climbing. He has nothing but his climbing shoes, his chalk bag, and the power of his mind. If he makes a mistake, he will die.

❷ Born in 1985, Alex started climbing when he was 11. Yosemite is by far his favorite place. A mecca for climbers, Yosemite has walls that are absolutely huge—and steep, like the 3,000 foot (about 1,000 m) wall of The Nose. Then there's Half Dome. Most serious climbers take a day or two to climb to the top, spending the night in tents clipped to the rock wall. Alex did it in two hours and 50 minutes, a new record, when he was just 23 years old.

❸ **While he is climbing, he wonders what he is doing there, why he is doing it.** Doubt is the climber's enemy. He has to believe he can do it. He might stall for a minute, then his confidence comes back and he does the impossible.

❹ **Taking risks is one way of finding out who you are, according to British climber, Johnny Dawes.** In his book, *Full of Myself*, he writes that climbing is a form of self-expression. Valuing a "genuine experience," he doesn't think highly of today's climbers who research the route and go over it again and again. That's "work."

●●英文を読む前に●●

1. 知っている単語に ☑ を入れる
2. 【半数以上知っている】
→英文を読み、知らない単語の意味を類推する
【半数以上わからない】
→単語の意味を辞書で調べてから英文を読む

- □ risky
- □ agile
- □ quick
- □ solo
- □ ultimate
- □ chalk
- □ by far
- Yosemite　ヨセミテ国立公園をさす
- □ mecca
- □ absolutely
- □ huge
- The Nose　ヨセミテ内のクライミングルートの１つ
- Half Dome　ヨセミテ内の巨大な花崗岩ドーム
- □ serious
- □ to spend
- □ to clip
- □ to wonder
- □ doubt
- □ enemy
- □ to stall
- □ confidence
- □ impossible
- □ to take risks
- □ to find out
- □ according to
- □ self-expression
- □ to value
- □ genuine
- □ route

Climbing should be an adventure. His famous climbs were all done "on sight"—no practice or prior knowledge. So far only Alex has been able to match his record climbs on the first attempt.

ハーフドームはヨセミテ国立公園を代表する観光スポットでもある。

- □ adventure
- □ prior
- □ knowledge
- □ so far
- □ to match
- □ attempt

Paragraph Reading

A. 第❶段落の太字の文の内容として、正しいものを選びましょう。

a. 危険なロッククライミング界のトップはアレックス・オノルドである。

b. 危険な岩の頂上にいるのはアレックス・オノルドである。

c. ロッククライミングは世界で一番危険だ。

B. 第❸段落の太字の文の内容として、正しいものを選びましょう。

a. 登山中、彼は自分のしていることに懐疑的になる。

b. 登山中、彼はこれからどうすればよいかわからなくなる。

c. 登山中、彼は頂上に着いたときに何をすべきかを考える。

C. 第❹段落の太字の文の内容として、正しいものを選びましょう。

a. ジョニー・ドーズによれば、ロッククライミングは自分を見失う危険がある。

b. 危険を冒すことで、自分が何者かがわかる。

c. イギリス人のロッククライミングは危険だ。

SECOND READING

Close Reading　wonder 疑問詞 S + V

[　　] 内の語句を並べ替えて文を完成させましょう。

1. He wonders [doing / he / is / there / what].

____

2. He wonders [doing / he / it / is / why].

____

3. I wonder [do the homework / how long / it / take / to / will].

____

POINT!

wonder の後に疑問詞（5W1H）で始まる節をつけて、「～だろうか／～かと（不思議に）思う」という意味の間接疑問文を作ることができる。

Unit 6 で学習したように、ふつうの（直接）疑問文では［be 動詞または do + S（主語）］の語順だが、間接疑問文では［S（主語）+ V（動詞）］と、肯定文と同じ語順になる。

（直接）疑問文

When will (V1) your brother (S) be (V2) back home?（あなたの兄さんはいつ帰宅しますか）

間接疑問文

I **wonder when** your brother (S) will be (V) back home.（あなたの兄さんはいつ帰宅するのでしょうか）

wonder 以外を使った関節疑問文の例として、以下のようなものがある。

I'm not **sure where** we (S) are going (V).（我々がどこに向かっているかは定かではありません）

I don't **know what time** the class (S) starts (V).（私は何時に授業が始まるのか知りません）

Reading Comprehension

本文の内容に合う文はT、合わないものはFを選びましょう。

1. フリーソロ・クライミングは、究極のロッククライミングだ。 [T / F]

2. 多くの登山家が1、2日かけて上がる崖をアレックスは約3時間で登った。 [T / F]

3. ジョニー・ドーズは綿密に下調べをしてから崖を登る。 [T / F]

Listening

DL 43 CD 1-43

①〜③の音声を聞き、それぞれの内容と合うものをa、bから選びましょう。

① **a.** 俊敏なアレックスは「フリーソロ・クライミング」と呼ばれるものをしている。
b. 俊敏さだけが「フリーソロ・クライミング」におけるアレックスの強味ではない。

② **a.** ヨセミテの絶壁は非常に広大だ。
b. ヨセミテが巨大な壁となって立ちはだかっている。

③ **a.** これまでの第1位の記録保持者はアレックスである。
b. これまでにアレックスだけがジョニー・ドーズに匹敵する記録を出せた。

① [ ] ② [ ] ③ [ ]

REFLECTION

Fill in the Blanks

DL 44 CD 1-44

1〜3の英文を聞き、空欄に語句を入れ文を完成させましょう。

1. If the climber ( ) ( ) ( ), he will die.

2. ( ) ( ) the climber's enemy.

3. ( ) ( ) ( ) ( ) he can do it.

Writing & Speaking

A. ［I wonder 疑問詞 + S + V］を使い、日本語に合うように［　］内の語句を並べ替えて①〜⑦の文を完成させましょう。

① 彼が何歳なのか（と思う）

I wonder ______________________________.

② 彼はいつフリークライミングを始めたのか（と思う）

I wonder ______________________________.

③ 雨はいつ止むのか（と思う）

I wonder ______________________________.

④ その壁はどのくらい急勾配だったのか（と思う）

I wonder ______________________________.

⑤ 彼はたいてい、どのくらいの速さで彼は崖を登るのか（と思う）

I wonder ______________________________.

⑥ 彼は今、何を考えているのか（と思う）

I wonder ______________________________.

⑦ 彼の旧友たちは今どこにいるのか（と思う）

I wonder ______________________________.

B. ペアを組み、①〜⑦について A さんは日本語を言い、B さんはそれに相当する英語を言いましょう。終わったら役割を交代して練習しましょう。

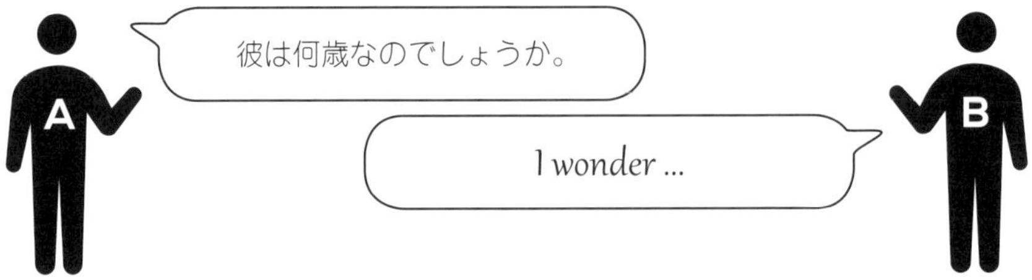

A
彼は何歳なのでしょうか。
I wonder ...
B

Unit 8 Fair Trade: *Helping People in Developing Countries*

LET'S START!

Guess What?

"Fair Trade: *Helping People in Developing Countries*" というタイトルから何に関する文章を予想しますか。

a. 途上国の生産者と環境を守る公正取引の話

b. 売上の一部が発展途上国の支援金となる電子マネーの話

c. 生活必需品を船で運んで発展途上国の人々を支援する基金の話

Check Words

A. 下線部の単語または語句の品詞に注意して、その意味を a ～ c から選びましょう。

1. When the market price for a farm product drops, farmers suffer.
a. 市場価値のある　**b.** スーパーの値段　**c.** 市場価格

2. Fair trade promises to buy products at a fair price that covers the cost of production even when market prices fall.
a. 生産コスト　**b.** 制作にかかる時間　**c.** 制作上の犠牲

3. Fair trade has helped people who had been living in poverty to lead a better life.
a. 自由の　**b.** 貧困　**c.** 貧しい

4. They are willing to pay a little extra for fair trade products.
a. 追加の金額　**b.** さらに上の　**c.** 特大の

5. The concept of fair trade has had a positive impact on producers in developing countries.
a. 先進国　**b.** 国が発展すること　**c.** 発展途上国

B. 上の 5 つの文は本文に登場するものです。これらの意味から考えて、**Guess What?** で立てた予想は正しいですか。間違っていれば、選び直しましょう。

FIRST READING

DL 45~49　CD 1-45 ~ CD 1-49

英文を読み、あとに続く問題に答えなさい。

❶ **When the market price for a farm product drops, farmers suffer. It is particularly difficult for farmers in developing countries where they get little or no help from the government.**

❷ Makandianfing Keita is a cotton farmer in Mali, a small country in western Africa, where cotton prices had gone down and down until they were below the cost of production. Keita had to spend more money on growing cotton than he got from selling it. He was a victim of the market price. He lives in an area where there was no healthcare, and children had to walk 10 kilometers to the nearest school.

❸ Keita was lucky, though. He and other cotton farmers of the village formed a co-op to become members of a fair trade organization called the Fairtrade Foundation in 2005. **Fair trade promises to buy products at a fair price that covers the cost of production even when market prices fall.** It also gives a 10% premium to the co-op to be used for education, healthcare, or farm improvements. With this money Keita's group built a school and a health clinic and installed a pump for drinking water.

❹ In hundreds of cases like these, fair trade has helped people who had been living in poverty to lead a better life. The Fairtrade mark can

●●英文を読む前に●●

1. 知っている単語に ☑ を入れる
2. 【半数以上知っている】
→英文を読み、知らない単語の意味を類推する
【半数以上わからない】
→単語の意味を辞書で調べてから英文を読む

- ☐ farm product
- ☐ to drop
- ☐ farmer
- ☐ to suffer
- ☐ particularly
- ☐ difficult
- ☐ government
- ☐ cotton
- ☐ to go down
- ☐ below
- ☐ to spend
- ☐ to sell
- ☐ victim
- ☐ an area
- ☐ healthcare
- ☐ though
- ☐ village
- ☐ to form
- ☐ co-op
- ☐ fair
- ☐ organization
- ☐ to promise
- ☐ to cover
- ☐ to fall
- ☐ premium
- ☐ improvement
- ☐ to install
- ☐ pump
- ☐ case
- ☐ to lead a life
- ☐ mark

be seen on thousands of products ranging from bananas from Ecuador to handmade baskets from Kenya. It is a certification that shows that the product has been produced according to the Fairtrade standards that protect workers and the environment.

❺ **Most people say they are willing to pay a little extra for fair trade products because the money goes to help the people who produce them.** On the other hand, critics say that many fair trade organizations are not transparent about their finances and that supporting prices is not a good solution. On the whole, however, the concept of fair trade has had a positive impact on producers in developing countries and has raised awareness of their problems among consumers in developed countries.

- ☐ to range from A to B
- ☐ Ecuador
- ☐ handmade
- ☐ basket
- ☐ certification
- ☐ according to
- ☐ standard
- ☐ to protect
- ☐ environment
- ☐ to be willing to do
- ☐ on the other hand
- ☐ critic
- ☐ transparent
- ☐ finances
- ☐ to support
- ☐ solution
- ☐ on the whole
- ☐ however
- ☐ concept
- ☐ positive
- ☐ to raise
- ☐ awareness
- ☐ consumer

Paragraph Reading

A. 第❶段落の太字の 2 つの文の内容として、正しいものを選びましょう。

a. 農作物の需要供給は、発展途上国では農家が決めている。

b. 発展途上国では政府の援助を受けられないため、多くの農家が市場で農作物を販売する。

c. 農作物の市場価格が下がると、特に発展途上国の農家が苦しむ。

B. 第❸段落の太字の文の内容として、正しいものを選びましょう。

a. フェアトレードは誰もが公正な値段で農作物を販売できる市場である。

b. フェアトレードでは、市場価格に関係なく農家が価格を決める。

c. フェアトレードにより、市場価格が下落した場合でも生産コストに応じた公正な値段で取引を行うことができる。

C. 第❺段落の太字の文の内容として、正しいものを選びましょう。

a. フェアトレードで支払うお金の一部は支援金として国連に送られる。

b. フェアトレードで生産物を売買するとき、多くの人々がチップを払うことにためらいがないと述べている。

c. 生産者を支援することになるという理由で、多くの人が、多少追加料金を払ってもフェアトレードの製品を購入したいと述べている。

SECOND READING

Close Reading 助動詞

英文の下線部の意味を a、b から選びましょう。

1. Children <u>had to walk 10 kilometers</u> to the nearest school.

a. 10 キロ歩かねばならなかった

b. 10 キロ歩いたかもしれない

2. The Fairtrade mark <u>can be seen on thousands of products</u>.

a. 何千もの製品を見るべきである

b. 何千もの製品に見られる

POINT!

助動詞は動詞に意味を付加するもので、must / will / should / may / can などがあります。

助動詞	意味	例
must	～しなければならない（義務）= have to	They must (= have to) work until late.（彼らは遅くまで働かなければならない）
	～に違いない（強い推量）	He must be our teacher.（彼は私たちの先生に違いありません）
will	～だろう（未来・推量・可能性）	It will rain this afternoon.（昼には雨が降るでしょう）
can	～できる（可能）	He can speak French and Spanish.（彼はフランス語とスペイン語を話せます）
should	～すべき（義務）	You should eat a lot of vegetables.（あなたは野菜をたくさん食べるべきです）
may	～かもしれない（推量）	He may be her brother.（彼は彼女の兄かもしれません）

Reading Comprehension

本文の内容に合う文はT、合わないものはFを選びましょう。

1. ケイタはフェアトレードを行う前、綿栽培で大儲けし、学校や病院を建てた。 [T / F]

2. フェアトレードは貧困にある人々がより良い暮らしを送れるよう支援してきた。 [T / F]

3. フェアトレードは発展途上国の生産者に良い影響を与え、先進国の人々の意識を変えた。 [T / F]

Listening

DL 50 CD 1-50

①〜③の音声を聞き、それぞれの内容と合うものをa、bから選びましょう。

① **a.** ケイタの場合、綿を売って得た収入より、栽培するのにかかる費用のほうが多かった。
b. ケイタはもっと収入を得るために綿を栽培し、売った。

② **a.** 彼は健康のために一番近い学校まで10キロの道のりを歩いた。
b. 病院等の施設もなく、学校からも遠い場所に彼は住んでいた。

③ **a.** エクアドルではバナナ、ケニヤではかごがフェアトレード商品として有名である。
b. フェアトレードのマークはバナナからかごに至るまで数多くの製品についている。

① [ ] ② [ ] ③ [ ]

REFLECTION

Fill in the Blanks

DL 51 CD 1-51

1〜3の英文を聞き、空欄に語句を入れ文を完成させましょう。

1. Fair trade gives a 10% premium ( ) ( ) used for education, ( ), or farm ( ).

2. Fair trade ( ) helped people who ( ) been living ( ) poverty.

3. The concept of fair trade ( ) had a positive ( ) on producers in ( ) countries.

Writing & Speaking

A. 本文で使われた「～にたくさんのお金を使う」ことを意味する spend a lot of money on ~ の表現を用いて、日本語に合うように①～⑤の英文を完成させましょう。

	誰は	お金を使った	何(に)
(例)	生活協同組合は The co-op	～にたくさんのお金を使った spent a lot of money on	新しい学校を建設すること building a new school.
①	私は	～にたくさんのお金を使う	私の携帯電話
②	彼は	～にたくさんのお金を使った	彼の車
③	彼女は	～にたくさんのお金を使うだろう	彼女の子供を教育すること
④	ジョンは	～にたくさんのお金を使った	彼の家族との旅行
⑤	メアリーは	～にたくさんのお金を使うことができる	自分自身の趣味

B. ペアを組み、①～⑤についてAさんは日本語を言い、Bさんはそれに相当する英語を言いましょう。終わったら役割を交代して練習しましょう。

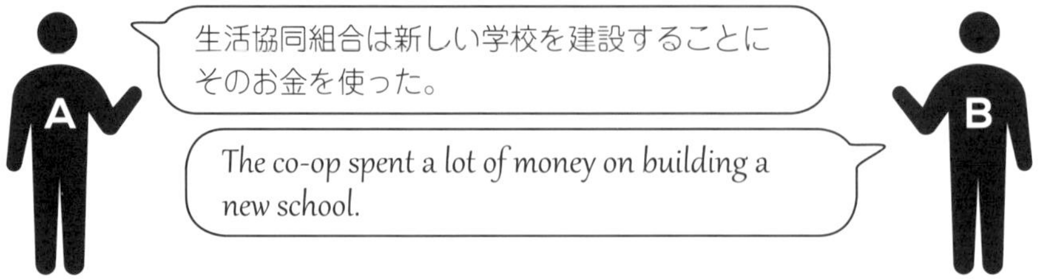

Unit 9 Caber Tossing: *A Macho Sport*

LET'S START!

Guess What?

"Caber Tossing: *A Macho Sport*" というタイトルから何に関する文章を予想しますか。

a. ケーブルカーを素手で動かす競技について

b. 筋肉の美しさを競うスポーツについて

c. 丸太を投げるスポーツ競技について

Check Words

A. 下線部の単語または語句の品詞に注意して、その意味を a ～ c から選びましょう。

1. I saw a program on TV about a traditional sports of Scotland.
a. 伝統　**b.** 伝統的な　**c.** 伝統的に

2. A big, muscular man was throwing a huge log as far as he could.
a. 筋肉　**b.** 筋骨たくましい　**c.** たくましく

3. A big, muscular man was throwing a huge log.
a. 丸太　**b.** 記録をつける　**c.** 木こり

4. A big, muscular man was throwing a huge log as far as he could.
a. 同じくらい長い　**b.** できるだけ遠くへ　**c.** はるか昔に

5 One requirement is that the contestant wears a kilt.
a. キルトスカート　**b.** ひざかけ　**c.** ナイフ

B. 上の 5 つの文は本文に登場するものです。これらの意味から考えて、**Guess What?** で立てた予想は正しいですか。間違っていれば、選び直しましょう。

FIRST READING

DL 52~55 CD 2-02 ~ CD 2-05

英文を読み、あとに続く問題に答えなさい。

❶ The other day I happened to see a program on TV about a traditional sport of Scotland. **A big, muscular man was carrying a huge log. He then threw it end over end.** The announcer said that this sport is called the caber toss. The logs are six to seven meters in length and weigh from 36 to 54 kilograms. Wow! The objective is to toss the log, or caber, so that it lands directly away from the "tosser" in the "12 o'clock" position.

❷ **I got really interested in this unusual sport and checked the Internet to find out about its origin.** There are several theories. The most likely is that during times of war—and there were many in the Scottish highlands—it often was necessary to quickly make a bridge over a stream. Being able to throw a log neatly across was a necessity when fleeing an enemy or chasing a rival. This is why the log is thrown for accuracy rather than for distance.

❸ **I also found out that Scots like to prove their skill in throwing lots of other things like rocks, cubes of metal, hammers, and bags of hay.** One event is like the Olympic shot put. Another is like the Olympic discus throw.

❹ These contests are usually held in the summer. Called the Highland Games, they are unique to Scotland and are considered national sports, as sumo is in Japan. Of course, they are very popular

●●英文を読む前に●●

1. 知っている単語に ☑ を入れる
2. 【半数以上知っている】
→英文を読み、知らない単語の意味を類推する
【半数以上わからない】
→単語の意味を辞書で調べてから英文を読む

- ☐ to happen to do
- ☐ program
- ☐ huge
- ☐ to throw
- ☐ end over end
- ☐ length
- ☐ to weigh
- ☐ objective
- ☐ to toss / tosser
- ☐ directly
- ☐ position
- ☐ to get interested
- ☐ to find out
- ☐ origin
- ☐ theory
- ☐ likely
- ☐ during
- ☐ highland
- ☐ necessary
- ☐ stream
- ☐ neatly
- ☐ accuracy
- ☐ distance
- ☐ cube
- ☐ metal
- ☐ hammer
- ☐ hay
- ☐ shot put
- ☐ discus throw
- ☐ contest / contestant
- ☐ to hold
- ☐ unique
- ☐ to consider
- ☐ popular / to popularize

in Scotland, but the Scots have popularized the Highland Games in other countries as well. In the United States, for example, they take place in many locations. There is bagpipe music, parades, good food, and sometimes sword fighting. One requirement is that the contestant wears a kilt. If you are in Scotland or the U.S. in the summer, try to schedule your trip so you can see the Highland Games. Actually there are Highland Games in Japan, too! Check it out!

- □ as well
- □ to take place
- □ location
- □ bagpipe
- □ parade
- □ sword
- □ requirement
- □ to check out
- □ to schedule
- □ actually

Paragraph Reading

A. 第❶段落の太字の２つの文の内容として、正しいものを選びましょう。

a. 筋肉質の大男が丸太の端を持って投げた。

b. 筋肉質の大男が丸太を上下に回転させて投げた。

c. 筋肉質の大男が巨大な丸太を担いでぐるぐる回った。

B. 第❷段落の太字の文の内容として、正しいものを選びましょう。

a. 私はこの不思議なスポーツはどこにでもある平凡なものだと思った。

b. 私はインターネットで偶然、この不思議なスポーツのことを知った。

c. 関心を持った私はインターネットでこの不思議なスポーツの由来を調べた。

C. 第❸段落の太字の文の内容として、正しいものを選びましょう。

a. スコットランドでは、生活の中でさまざまなものを投げる習慣がある。

b. スコットランドには、物を投げる技術を競うスポーツがいくつかある。

c. ケイバー・トスでは、丸太のほかに石やハンマーを投げることがある。

SECOND READING

Close Reading 受動態

次の文を受動態にしたものとして正しいものをａ～ｄから選びましょう。

1. People call this sport the Caber Toss.

a. This sport called people the Caber Toss.

b. This sport is called people the Caber Toss.

c. This sport is called the Caber Toss.

d. This sport called the Caber Toss by people.

2. They hold these contests in the summer.

a. These contests are holded in the summer.

b. These contests is holded in the summer.

c. These contests are held in the summer.

d. These contests is held in the summer.

POINT!

「S（主語）がV（動詞）する」という能動態に対し、「S（主語）がV（動詞）される」と受け身を意味する場合（受動態）は［be動詞＋過去分詞］で表します。

動作を「誰がした」ということよりも「誰にされた」のか、つまり動作を受けた方がより重要な場合は、それを主語にした受動態の文が使われます。

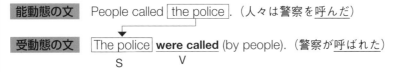

能動態の文　People called the police.（人々は警察を呼んだ）

受動態の文　The police **were called** (by people).（警察が呼ばれた）
S　V

(be動詞＋過去分詞形)

※受動態のbe動詞は、主語と時制に応じて、am, is, are, was, wereなど適切な形を選びます。

※受動態の場合、動作を「した」方（＝能動態の主語。上の問題のpeopleやthey）は省略されることがよくあります。

Reading Comprehension

本文の内容に合う文はT、合わないものはFを選びましょう。

1. ケイバー・トスは丸太を投げるスコットランドの伝統的なスポーツだ。 [T / F]

2. ケイバー・トスはスコットランドでしか見られない。 [T / F]

3. ケイバー・トスでは、プレーヤーはキルト・スカートを着用しなければならない。 [T / F]

Listening

DL 56 CD 2-06

①～③の音声を聞き、それぞれの内容と合うものをa、bから選びましょう。

① **a.** このスポーツの目的は、投げた丸太が12時ちょうどに垂直に立つかどうかを競うことである。
b. このスポーツの目的は、投げた丸太の上部が手前になり、投手に対して垂直に倒れたかを競うことである。

② **a.** 敵から逃れるとき、丸太をきちんと並べて川に橋をかける必要があった。
b. 遠くの敵に大きな丸太を投げつけられる力が必要とされた。

③ **a.** ハイランド・ゲームはスコットランドの国技とされている。
b. ハイランド・ゲーム愛好家は日本の相撲が好きだ。

① [ ] ② [ ] ③ [ ]

REFLECTION

Fill in the Blanks

DL 57 CD 2-07

1～3の英文を聞き、空欄に語句を入れ文を完成させましょう。

1. The announcer ( ) ( ) this sport is ( ) the caber toss.

2. This is why the log ( ) ( ) for accuracy ( ) ( ) for distance.

3. These contests ( ) ( ) in the summer and ( ) ( ) in many locations.

Writing & Speaking

A. 下の表の単語と語順を参考に、①～④の文を、受動態を使って英語で表現してみましょう。

	誰が	どうされる	付加情報
①	Two sumo wrestlers (2 人の力士)	call (名前を呼ばれた)	the judge (行司)によって
②	A few minutes (数分)	give (与えられた)	practice (練習)のために
③	Their match (対戦)	view (観られた)	a large audience (多くの観客)によって
④	An award (ある賞)	give (与えられた)	the winner (勝者)に

① Two sumo wrestlers ______________________________

______________________________.

② A few minutes ______________________________

______________________________.

③ Their match ______________________________

______________________________.

④ An award ______________________________

______________________________.

B. ペアを組み、①～④についてAさんは日本語を言い、Bさんはそれに相当する英語を言いましょう。終わったら役割を交代して練習しましょう。

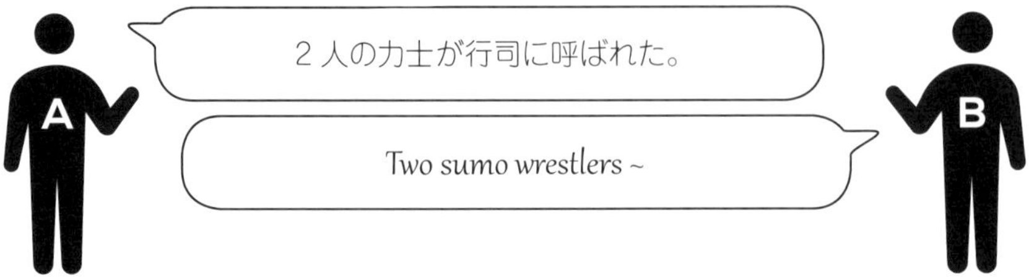

A
2 人の力士が行司に呼ばれた。
Two sumo wrestlers ~
B

Unit 10 Bacteria: *Small Things Doing a Big Job*

LET'S START!

Guess What?

"Bacteria: *Small Things Doing a Big Job*" というタイトルから何に関する文章を予想しますか。

a. 小さいが生命力の強い細菌の話

b. 人の体内で巨大化する細菌の話

c. 小さな活動が大きな貢献となった細菌の話

Check Words

A. 下線部の単語または語句の品詞に注意して、その意味を a ～ c から選びましょう。

1. If you are in good health, your <u>digestive system</u> is home to more than a hundred trillion bacteria.

a. 消化の良い　**b.** ダイエットシステム　**c.** 消化システム

2. Many actually are <u>beneficial</u>.

a. 有益な　**b.** 利益　**c.** 効果的な

3. Within two days the friendly bacteria have <u>multiplied</u> and replaced C. difficile.

a. 増やすための　**b.** 掛け算された　**c.** 増殖した

4. Bacteria are also put to work to <u>decompose</u> compost, garbage, and sewage.

a. 分解する　**b.** 分解された　**c.** 圧縮する

5. Miners now are using bacteria to <u>extract metals</u> from ores that have even only 1 percent of metal.

a. 金属を平たくする　**b.** 金属を抽出する　**c.** 抜き書きを作る

B. 上の 5 つの文は本文に登場するものです。これらの意味から考えて、**Guess What?** で立てた予想は正しいですか。間違っていれば、選び直しましょう。

FIRST READING

DL 58~62 CD 2-08 ~ CD 2-12

英文を読み、あとに続く問題に答えなさい。

❶ Right now, if you are in good health, your digestive system is home to more than a hundred trillion bacteria. Ugh! you say. **Fortunately, however, most bacteria are harmless. Many actually are beneficial, unlike viruses.** So far no virus that could be beneficial to humans has been found.

❷ On the contrary, viruses have caused human beings much misery. Smallpox, for example, killed 60 million people in Europe in the 18th century alone. Brought to the Americas by Europeans, it decimated the native population and thus enabled a few Spaniards to conquer the magnificent Aztec and Inca empires. Thankfully, smallpox recently has been eradicated by a global vaccination campaign.

❸ **Back to the beneficial bacteria: here is an example of what happens when you lose your little friends down there in your intestines, the ones that help with your digestion.** Now, if you have a bad infection and take a strong dose of antibiotics, all the good guys can get killed, as well as the bad guys that had caused the infection. Then it is possible for a nasty fellow called Clostridium difficile to take over. This bacterium causes awful diarrhea, and it is very difficult to get rid of.

❹ Recently, however, success has been found

●●英文を読む前に●●

1. 知っている単語に ☑ を入れる
2. 【半数以上知っている】
→英文を読み、知らない単語の意味を類推する
【半数以上わからない】
→単語の意味を辞書で調べてから英文を読む

- □ right now
- □ trillion
- □ bacteria
- □ fortunately
- □ harmless
- □ unlike
- □ virus
- □ on the contrary
- □ human beings
- □ misery
- □ smallpox
- □ to decimate
- □ native
- □ thus
- □ Spaniard
- □ to conquer
- □ magnificent

Aztec and Inca empires アステカとインカ帝国

- □ to eradicate
- □ vaccination
- □ back to
- □ intestine
- □ digestion
- □ infection
- □ to take a dose
- □ antibiotics
- □ nasty

Clostridium difficile クロストリジウム・ディフィシル（菌）

- □ to take over
- □ awful
- □ diarrhea
- □ to get rid of

with an unorthodox treatment. A sample of stool from a person in good health is put into the patient's large intestine. Within two days the friendly bacteria have multiplied and replaced C. difficile. It sounds icky, but it works. This procedure is called "faecal transplant", but most people call it "trans-poo-sion (transfusion + poo)".

❺ **Bacteria are also used to decompose compost, garbage, and sewage.** Miners now are using bacteria to extract metals from ores. Nearly 20 percent of the world's copper comes from biomining, and production has doubled since the mid-1990s. So don't diss bacteria. They are good for you.

☐ unorthodox
☐ treatment
☐ stool
☐ to put into
☐ to replace
☐ icky
☐ procedure
☐ faecal
☐ transplant
☐ transfusion
to poo（幼児語で）うんち
☐ compost
☐ garbage
☐ sewage
☐ miner
☐ ore
☐ copper
biomining バイオマイニング（菌を利用した採掘技術）
to diss（スラングで）けなす

Paragraph Reading

A. 第❶段落の太字の 2 つの文の内容として、正しいものを選びましょう。

a. 細菌の多くはウイルスと違って有益である。

b. 細菌の多くが無害なのは人にとって幸運な偶然である。

c. 細菌は有害だが、ウイルスは無害である。

B. 第❸段落の太字の文の内容として、正しいものを選びましょう。

a. 細菌は胃の中で消化をコントロールしている。

b. 消化を助ける細菌がいなくなるとどうなるかの例をみてみよう。

c. ある例によれば、子どものお腹には細菌がいて消化を助けているという。

C. 第❺段落の太字の文の内容として、正しいものを選びましょう。

a. 細菌はごみを分解して下水に流すことに使われる。

b. 細菌はごみや汚水を凝縮する。

c. 細菌は堆肥、ごみ、汚水を分解することにも使われる。

SECOND READING

Close Reading 現在完了

英文の下線部の意味を a、b から選びましょう。

1. Smallpox recently has been eradicated by a global vaccination campaign.

a. 天然痘は近年根絶された

b. 天然痘を最近根絶したことがある

2. Success has been found with an unorthodox treatment.

a. 成功がずっと続いている

b. 成功例が発見された

3. Production has doubled since the mid-1990s.

a. 生産量は二倍に達した

b. 生産量は二倍になりつつある

POINT!

形	have (has) ＋過去分詞
意味	動作や状態や出来事が、現在までに完了・経験した、もしくは継続していることを表す

完了　I **have finished** writing my essay.（エッセイを書き終えた）

経験　**Have** you ever **been** there?（そこに行ったことがありますか）
— Yes, I **have been** there twice.（ええ、２回行ったことがあります）
No, I **have** never **been** there.（いいえ、一度も行ったことはありません）

継続　I **have known** her since we were children.（私は子供の頃から彼女を知っている）

Reading Comprehension

本文の内容に合う文はT、合わないものはFを選びましょう。

1. 天然痘がヨーロッパ人によってアメリカ大陸に持ち込まれたとき、多くの先住民族が亡くなった。 [T / F]

2. 強い薬によって良い細菌まで死滅すると、下痢を引き起こす細菌などが増える。 [T / F]

3. 細菌は金属を食べるため、採掘現場では滅菌消毒が行われる。 [T / F]

Listening

DL 63　CD 2-13

①～③の音声を聞き、それぞれの内容と合うものをa、bから選びましょう。

① **a.** 今、100兆以上の細菌を食べると健康になると言われている。
b. 今、健康な身体には100兆以上の細菌がいる。

② **a.** そして、クロストリジウム・ディフィシルは悪質な菌に乗っ取られる可能性が出てくる。
b. すると、クロストリジウム・ディフィシルと呼ばれる意地悪な仲間は乗っ取ることができるようになる。

③ **a.** 多少かゆくても働かなくてはいけない。
b. 嫌な感じだが、うまくいく。

① [　　　] ② [　　　] ③ [　　　]

REFLECTION

Fill in the Blanks

DL 64　CD 2-14

1～3の英文を聞き、空欄に語句を入れ文を完成させましょう。

1. (　　) (　　　　　) no virus that could be beneficial to humans (　　　　　) (　　　　　) (　　　　　).

2. (　　　　　) two days the friendly bacteria (　　　　　) (　　　　　) and (　　　　　　　) the bad bacteria.

3. Production (　　) doubled (　　　　　) the mid-(　　　　　).

Writing & Speaking

A. 本文で使われた「～するとき何が起こるか」を意味する what happens when~ の表現を用いて、日本語に合うように①～③の英文を完成させましょう。

	何がどうする	何が起こるか	～ときに
(例)	Here is an example of (これが例である)	what happens	when you lose a lot of bacteria (たくさんの細菌を失う)
①	I can easily guess (私は容易に予測できる)		(あなたが徹夜をする)
②	You should think of (あなたが考えるべきだ)		(旅行を計画する)
③	I know (私にはわかる)		(子どもたちが自分たちの携帯を持つ)

(例) Here is an example of what happens when you lose a lot of bacteria.
(これがたくさんの細菌を失うときに何が起こるかの例である)

① I can easily guess ____

____.

② You should think of ____

____.

③ I know ____

____.

B. ペアを組み、①～③についてAさんは日本語を言い、Bさんはそれに相当する英語を言いましょう。終わったら役割を交代して練習しましょう。

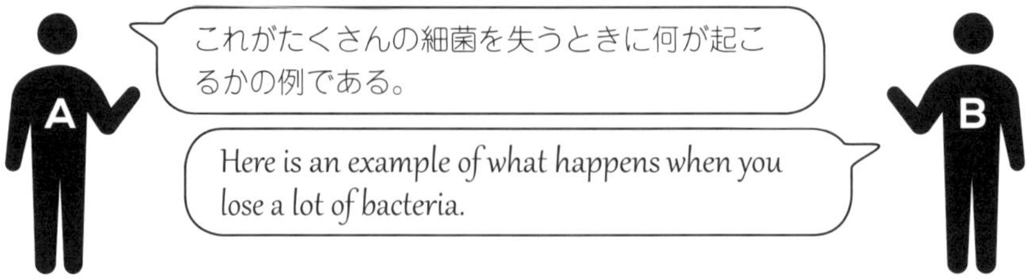

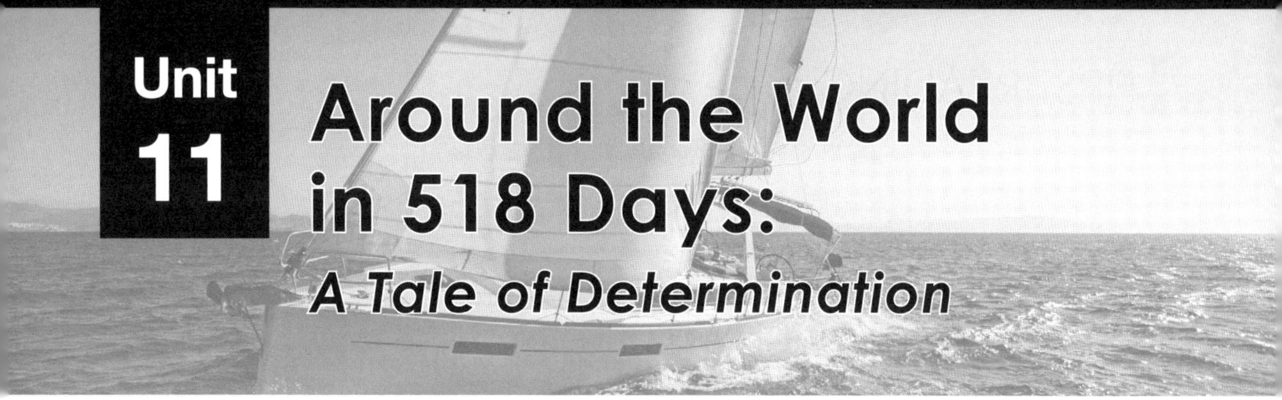

Unit 11 Around the World in 518 Days: *A Tale of Determination*

LET'S START!

Guess What?

"Around the World in 518 Days: *A Tale of Determination*" というタイトルから何に関する文章を予想しますか。

a. 518 日間世界中を旅することで生まれた、ある決意について

b. 518 日を周期とする天体を発見した船乗りの話

c. 自分の意志でやろうと決めて、518 日で世界一周した話

Check Words

A. 下線部の単語または語句の品詞に注意して、その意味を a ～ c から選びましょう。

1. Laura Decker became <u>the youngest person</u> to complete a solo voyage around the world. **a.** 若かった **b.** 最も若い人 **c.** 若者

2. Laura, who is from the Netherlands, is the ninth in a series of young <u>sailors</u> sailing around the world alone. **a.** 船乗り **b.** 船を操る **c.** 舟型の

3. Laura was determined to <u>go ahead</u> with her plans.
a. 進められた **b.** 進める **c.** 任せる

4. Laura's journey took her through the Panama Canal, <u>across the Pacific Ocean</u>.
a. 太平洋の海上を **b.** 太平洋の向かいに **c.** 太平洋を横切って

5. At sea I felt comfortable and relaxed, especially during the long <u>crossing</u> of the Indian and Atlantic Oceans. **a.** 渡航 **b.** 交差点 **c.** 横切るために

B. 上の 5 つの文は本文に登場するものです。これらの意味から考えて、**Guess What?** で立てた予想は正しいですか。間違っていれば、選び直しましょう。

FIRST READING

DL 65~69　CD 2-15 ~ CD 2-19

英文を読み、あとに続く問題に答えなさい。

❶ **When Laura Dekker sailed her boat into the harbor of St. Maarten in the Dutch Antilles on January 21, 2012, she became the youngest person to complete a solo voyage around the world.** She was exactly 16 years and four months old.

❷ Laura, who is from the Netherlands, is the ninth in a series of young sailors sailing around the world alone. The first was Robin Lee Graham, who left Los Angeles on July 27, 1965 when he had just turned 16. His voyage had been risky: he had almost been killed when a huge ship barely missed his boat one night. His voyage created a sensation and was written up in *National Geographic*.

❸ **Laura started her voyage when she was barely 15. Although her parents supported her wish, Dutch authorities blocked her trip because, they said, she was too young to risk her life.** Also, by law she should stay in school. However, Laura was determined to go ahead with her plans. She had been born on a yacht off the coast of New Zealand when her parents were on a seven-year voyage around the world. She got her own boat when she was six.

❹ Laura's journey took her through the Panama Canal, across the Pacific Ocean, across the Indian Ocean, past the stormy Cape of Good Hope, and

●●英文を読む前に●●

1. 知っている単語に ☑ を入れる
2. 【半数以上知っている】→英文を読み、知らない単語の意味を類推する
【半数以上わからない】→単語の意味を辞書で調べてから英文を読む

- ☐ to sail
- ☐ harbor
- the Dutch Antilles　オランダ領アンティル
- ☐ to complete
- ☐ solo
- ☐ voyage
- ☐ exactly
- ☐ the Netherlands
- ☐ in a series of ~
- ☐ alone
- ☐ to turn
- ☐ risky
- ☐ almost
- ☐ huge
- ☐ barely
- ☐ to miss
- ☐ to create a sensation
- *National Geographic*　『ナショナルジオグラフィック』誌
- ☐ wish
- ☐ authorities
- ☐ to block
- ☐ to risk
- ☐ by law
- ☐ determined to do
- ☐ off the coast
- ☐ the Panama Canal
- ☐ the Pacific Ocean
- ☐ the Indian Ocean
- ☐ the Cape of Good Hope

then across the Atlantic Ocean. Along the way she stopped at the Galapagos Islands, Tahiti, Tonga, Fiji and Darwin, Australia. "At sea I felt comfortable and relaxed, especially during the long crossing of the Indian and Atlantic Oceans," she said in perfect English.

❺ **After 518 days and a lot of dangerous and scary moments, she arrived home safely with the kind of knowledge that she never could have got at school.**

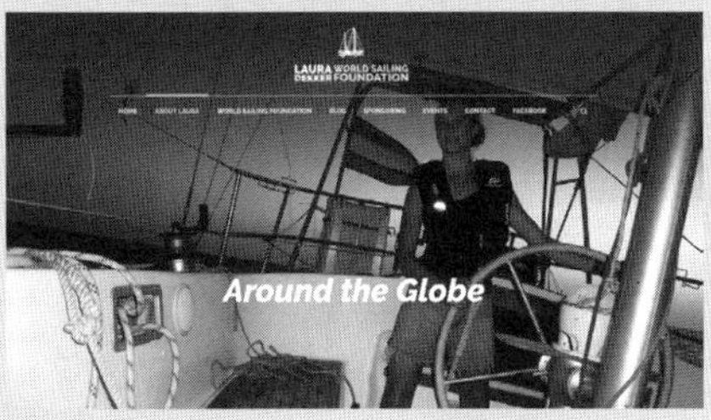

Laura Dekkerのオフィシャルサイト（https://lauradekkerworldsailingfoundation.com/）では世界一周渡航の詳細やルートなどを閲覧することができる。

- ☐ the Atlantic Ocean
- ☐ comfortable
- ☐ relaxed
- ☐ especially
- ☐ dangerous
- ☐ scary
- ☐ moment
- ☐ to arrive
- ☐ safely
- ☐ knowledge
- ☐ never

Paragraph Reading

A. 第❶段落の太字の文の内容として、正しいものを選びましょう。

a. ローラは単独ヨットによる世界一周を最年少で終えた。

b. ローラは 2012 年オランダに到着し、世界一周旅行を始めた。

c. ローラはヨットで世界一周の旅に出かけることで若返った。

B. 第❸段落の太字の 2 つの文の内容として、正しいものを選びましょう。

a. ローラの両親はローラの意思を尊重したが、周りの人々は様々な手段を講じて彼女の旅を妨害した。

b. ローラは 15 歳で世界一周の旅にでかけたが、両親とオランダ政府から反対された。

c. ローラは 15 歳で世界一周をしようと計画したが、オランダ政府は若すぎるといって反対した。

C. 第❺段落の太字の文の内容として、正しいものを選びましょう。

a. ローラは航海の間も勉強を続けたため、家に帰ったとき学校の勉強についていくことができた。

b. 世界一周の旅を終え、ローラは学校で学ぶことのできない知識を得て無事に家に帰った。

c. 518 日の旅を終えてローラは無事に家に帰ったが、その間学校で勉強することはできなかった。

SECOND READING

Close Reading 過去完了

次の下線部の意味を a、b から選びましょう。

1. The first was Robin Lee Graham, who left Los Angeles on July 27, 1965 when he had just turned 16.

a. 彼は 16 歳になったばかりだった　**b.** 彼はもうすぐ 16 歳になるところだ。

2. He had almost been killed when a huge ship barely missed his boat one night.

a. 彼はすでに死んでいた　**b.** 彼はもう少しで死ぬところだった

POINT!

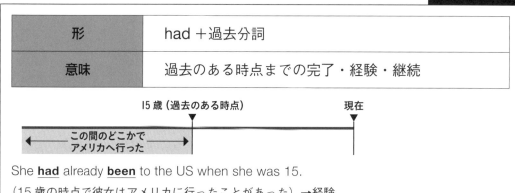

形	had ＋過去分詞
意味	過去のある時点までの完了・経験・継続

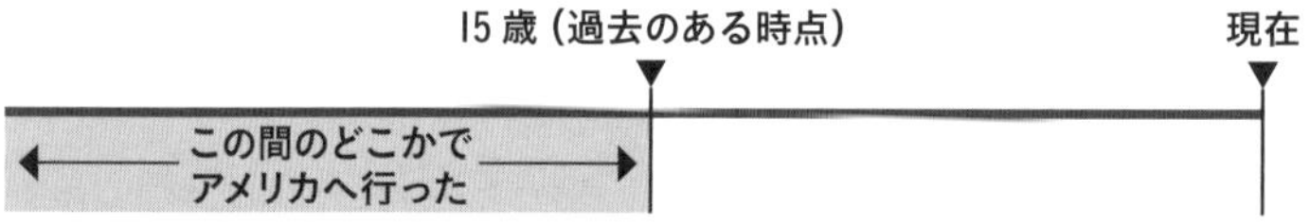

She **had** already **been** to the US when she was 15.
（15 歳の時点で彼女はアメリカに行ったことがあった）→経験

（その他の例）
The meeting **hadn't finished** when Betsy came into the room.
（ベッツィが部屋に入ってきたとき、まだ会議は終わっていなかった）→完了（否定）
My father **had been** in the hospital three months before he had his cancer operation.
（私の父はガンの手術をするまでに３ヶ月入院していた）→継続

Reading Comprehension

本文の内容に合う文はT、合わないものはFを選びましょう。

1. ロビン・リー・グレアムが16歳で世界一周したとき、その話はセンセーションを巻き起こした。 [T / F]

2. ローラ・デッカーの両親はヨットに乗ったことはなかった。 [T / F]

3. ローラはインド洋や喜望峰などを周り、途中様々な国に立ち寄った。 [T / F]

Listening

DL 70 CD 2-20

①〜③の音声を聞き、それぞれの内容と合うものをa、bから選びましょう。

① **a.** 法律により、彼女は学校に送り返されることとなった。
b. 法律では、彼女は学校に通っていなければならない。

② **a.** 6歳のとき、彼女は自分の船を持った。
b. 彼女が初めて船に乗ったのは6歳のときである。

③ **a.** ローラの旅は大西洋からパナマ運河を通り、最後に太平洋を渡るというものだった。
b. ローラはパナマ運河や太平洋、インド洋、大西洋をまわった。

① [　　] ② [　　] ③ [　　]

REFLECTION

Fill in the Blanks

DL 71 CD 2-21

1〜3の英文を聞き、空欄に語句を入れ文を完成させましょう。

1. He (　　　) Los Angeles when he (　　　) just (　　　) 16.

2. His voyage (　　　) (　　　) risky; he had almost (　　　) (　　　).

3. She (　　　) (　　　) (　　　) on (　　　) yacht off the coast (　　　) New Zealand.

Writing & Speaking

A. 本文中に出て来た過去完了の表現を参考に、①～④の文を日本語に合うように書いてみましょう。①～③はヒントを提示していますが、④はすべて自分で考えて作文してみましょう。

	誰が	どうした	～したときに（過去のある時点）
①	My sister （私の姉）	turn nineteen（19 歳になる） →ちょうど（just）なったばかりだった	アメリカに引っ越したとき → move to「～へ引っ越す」
②	His life （彼の人生）	be risky（危険である） →ずっと危険であった	アメリカへ引っ越す前は → before「～の前に」
③	The Civil War （南北戦争）	break out（起きた） →すでに起きていた	私の祖母が生まれたときには → grandmother「祖母」
④	私の父は運転免許を取ったとき、18 歳になったばかりだった。		

① My sister ______________________________

______________________________ when she moved to the United States.

② His life ______________________________

before he ______________________________.

③ The Civil War ______________________________

when ______________________________.

④ ______________________________

______________________________.

B. ペアを組み、①～④について A さんは日本語を言い、B さんはそれに相当する英語を言いましょう。終わったら役割を交代して練習しましょう。

Unit 12 Kodak and Apple: *A Tale of Two Companies*

LET'S START!

Guess What?

"Kodak and Apple: *A Tale of Two Companies*" というタイトルから何に関する文章を予想しますか。

a. 二人の仲間の物語

b. 二つの企業の栄枯盛衰

c. 二つの企業を巡る歴史小説

Check Words

A. 下線部の単語または語句の品詞に注意して、その意味をa～cから選びましょう。

1. In January 2012 Kodak filed for <u>bankruptcy</u>.
a. 倒産　**b.** 銀行　**c.** 銀行のような

2. The company was founded by George Eastman to produce the world's first flexible roll <u>film</u>.　**a.** 映画　**b.** ファイル　**c.** フィルム

3. Among Kodak's <u>innovations</u> was Kodachrome, the best slide and motion picture film in the world.　**a.** 新技術　**b.** 新しく作る　**c.** 革新的な

4. Digital cameras then <u>undermined</u> the photo film industry.
a. 活性化された　**b.** 内蔵する　**c.** 弱体化させた

5. One of Steve Jobs' greatest gifts was his ability to see the future and to <u>turn innovation into success</u>, like the computer mouse.
a. 新技術を成功させる　**b.** 新技術の成功につまづく　**c.** 新たな成功に近づく

B. 上の5つの文は本文に登場するものです。これらの意味から考えて、**Guess What?** で立てた予想は正しいですか。間違っていれば、選び直しましょう。

FIRST READING

DL 72~75 CD 2-22 ~ CD 2-25

英文を読み、あとに続く問題に答えなさい。

❶ **In 2012, Kodak filed for bankruptcy. It was a sad end to one of the greatest companies in the United States.** The Kodak trademark dates back to 1888. The company was founded by George Eastman to produce the world's first flexible roll film. In 1900, its easy-to-use one-dollar Brownie camera became an overnight craze. Eastman was very good to his employees. He pioneered profit-sharing and gave generous wage dividends.

❷ Among Kodak's innovations was Kodachrome, the best slide and motion picture film in the world. Kodak also created the first digital camera in 1975; however, it didn't want to give up its reliance on film. This allowed rivals like Canon and Sony to take over the market. Digital cameras then undermined the photo film industry. In effect, Kodak had created the technology that killed it.

❸ **Steve Jobs, the founder of Apple, on the other hand, never stopped innovating and pioneering.** In 1976 when he was just 21, he started out with his friend Steve Wozniak to create a mass-market computer. They called it Apple. One of Jobs' greatest gifts was his ability to see the future and to turn innovation into success, like the computer mouse. Xerox had made the prototype but didn't realize its potential. Jobs

●●英文を読む前に●●

1. 知っている単語に ☑ を入れる
2. 【半数以上知っている】→英文を読み、知らない単語の意味を類推する
【半数以上わからない】→単語の意味を辞書で調べてから英文を読む

- ☐ to file
- ☐ sad
- ☐ company
- ☐ trademark
- ☐ to date back
- ☐ to found
- ☐ to produce
- ☐ flexible
- ☐ easy-to-use
- ☐ overnight
- ☐ craze
- ☐ good to
- ☐ employee
- ☐ to pioneer
- ☐ profit-sharing
- ☐ generous
- ☐ wage dividend
- ☐ reliance on ~
- ☐ to allow ~ to do
- ☐ to take over
- ☐ market
- ☐ industry
- ☐ in effect
- ☐ founder
- ☐ to innovate
- ☐ to start out
- ☐ mass-market
- ☐ ability
- ☐ mouse
- ☐ prototype
- ☐ to realize
- ☐ potential

did. His new computer, the Mac, was the first to use a mouse. His insistence on a simplified user interface has made Apple computers, the iPod, the iPad, and finally the iPhone take the lead in each field.

❹ Even when Jobs lost his position at Apple, he turned that failure into a huge success by founding Pixar, the animated film company that produced *Toy Story*, *Monsters, Inc*, and *Finding Nemo*. **When Jobs died of cancer in October 2011, the whole world mourned, not because he was a billionaire, but because he was an inspiration to all.**

- ☐ the first to use ~
- ☐ insistence on ~
- ☐ to simplify
- ☐ interface
- ☐ to take the lead in ~
- ☐ field
- ☐ position
- ☐ failure
- ☐ huge
- ☐ animated
- ☐ to die of ~
- ☐ cancer
- ☐ billionaire
- ☐ to mourn

Paragraph Reading

A. 第❶段落の太字の 2 つの文の内容として、正しいものを選びましょう。

a. コダックは銀行にファイルを提出し、悲しい倒産を締めくくった。

b. アメリカ屈指の大企業の一つ、コダック社は 2012 年に倒産した。

c. コダックの倒産は、アメリカの企業家たちにとって悲しいことだ。

B. 第❸段落の太字の文の内容として、正しいものを選びましょう。

a. アップル社の創設者は革新も開拓もしなかった。

b. スティーブ・ジョブズは技術の革新と開拓を行い続けた。

c. スティーブ・ジョブズとアップル社の創設者は今なお働いている。

C. 第❹段落の太字の文の内容として、正しいものを選びましょう。

a. 新しい時代が始まり、ジョブズは億万長者になった。

b. ジョブズが人々にインスピレーションを与えることで新時代が始まった。

c. 人々は皆にインスピレーションを与えたジョブスの死を悲しんだ。

SECOND READING

Close Reading 否定を意味する not

英文の下線部の意味を a、b から選びましょう。

1. However, the company didn't want to give up its reliance on film.

a. その会社はフィルムへの依存をやめようとはしなかった

b. その会社はフィルムへの依存をやめたかった

2. When Jobs died of cancer in October 2011, the whole world mourned, not because he was a billionaire, but because he was an inspiration to all.

a. 彼は億万長者ではなかったが、人々にインスピレーションを与えたから

b. 彼が億万長者だからではなく、人々にインスピレーションを与えたから

POINT!

not は「〜でない」という否定を意味します。否定しようとする名詞や節の前に not をつけたり、動詞の前に（be 動詞の場合は後ろ）do/does/did ＋ not をつけて表します。

名詞を否定する場合 ＝ not ＋名詞

It is not a pencil, but a pen.（それは鉛筆ではなくペンです）

※ not A but B で「A ではなく B」

動詞を否定する場合（一般動詞） ＝ do/does/did ＋ not ＋動詞

You do not (don't) know my sister's name.（あなたは私の姉の名前を知りません）

He did not (didn't) buy it.（彼はそれを買いませんでした）

動詞を否定する場合（be 動詞） ＝ be 動詞＋ not

I'm not Nick.（私はニックではありません）

節を否定する場合 ＝ not ＋節

Do you have any better plan?（何かもっと良いプランはありますか）

— Not that I can think of.（考えるかぎりないですね）

※前述の not A but B も A、B を節にして用いることができる⇒上の設問 2

Reading Comprehension

本文の内容に合う文はT、合わないものはFを選びましょう。

1. コダック社は優れた映画用フィルムとデジタルカメラを開発した。 [T / F]

2. ジョブズは革新的な技術を考案したが実用化できなかった。 [T / F]

3. アップル社の製品は使い勝手が良くないが売れ行きが良い。 [T / F]

Listening

DL 76 CD 2-26

①〜③の音声を聞き、それぞれの内容と合うものをa、bから選びましょう。

① **a.** 1900年の時点で1ドルで買えるブローニー・カメラは一晩中使うことができた。
b. 1900年、ブローニー・カメラは突如として大流行した。

② **a.** これにより、キャノンやソニーなどのライバル会社に市場を奪われた。
b. これにより、キャノンやソニーなどのライバル会社が市場参入を果たした。

③ **a.** 彼はピクサーを設立し、失敗を成功に変えた。
b. 彼の成功はピクサー設立によって失敗に転じた。

① [ ] ② [ ] ③ [ ]

REFLECTION

Fill in the Blanks

DL 77 CD 2-27

1〜3の英文を聞き、空欄に語句を入れ文を完成させましょう。

1. Kodak was ( ) by George Eastman ( ) produce the world's ( ) flexible roll ( ).

2. One ( ) Steve Jobs' greatest gifts was his ability ( ) see the future and ( ) turn innovation ( ) success.

3. Xerox ( ) made the ( ) but didn't ( ) its potential.

Writing & Speaking

A. 本文で使われた「～しはじめる／～するのをやめる」を意味する start -ing / stop -ing の表現を用いて、日本語に合うように①～③の英文を完成させましょう。

	誰が	どうする	何を
(例)	Steve Jobs (スティーブ・ジョブズは)	never stopped (決してやめなかった)	pursue new technology (新しいテクノロジーを追求する)
①	(私は)	(はじめたい)	do something new (何か新しいことをする)
②	(あなたは)	(やめるべきだ)	watch YouTube (ユーチューブを観る)
③	(彼女は)	(はじめた)	think about global warming (地球温暖化について考える)

(例) Steve Jobs never stopped pursuing new technology.
(スティーブ・ジョブズは新しいテクノロジーを追求することを決してやめなかった)

① ______________________________

____

② ______________________________

____

③ ______________________________

____

B. ペアを組み、①～③についてAさんは日本語を言い、Bさんはそれに相当する英語を言いましょう。終わったら役割を交代して練習しましょう。

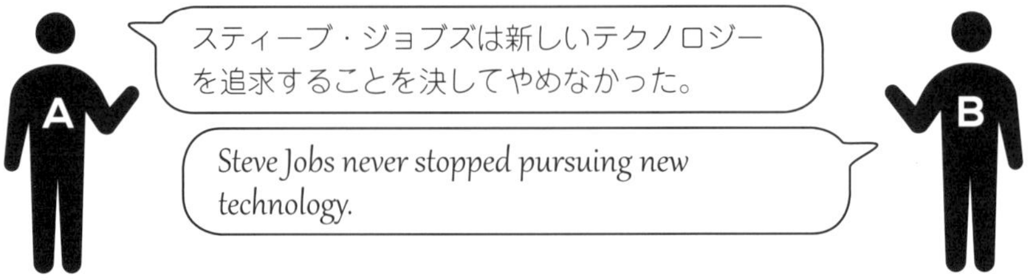

Unit 13 Happy Endings: *What Do People Want in a Movie?*

LET'S START!

Guess What?

"Happy Endings: *What Do People Want in a Movie?*" というタイトルから何に関する文章を予想しますか。

a. ハッピーエンドの映画は必ずヒットする

b. 観客が求めるのはどんな結末の映画か

c. ハッピーエンドの映画が好きな人の多い国はどこか

Check Words

A. 下線部の単語または語句の品詞に注意して、その意味をa～cから選びましょう。

1. People should have mood-elevating movies.
a. 気分を落ち込ませる　**b.** 気持ちを高揚させる　**c.** 気持ちを慰める

2. Deciding to find out what kind of movies make people happy, she analyzed box-office hits.　**a.** 分析　**b.** 分析された　**c.** 分析した

3. The lead character winning at the end of the movie is not the most important element.　**a.** 主人公　**b.** 鉛の性質　**c.** リーダー気質

4. Audiences care about the positive resolution of those relationships.
a. 解決　**b.** 解決する　**c.** 解決の

5. After the Karate Kid wipes out his opponent, he makes peace with him.
a. ～と平穏に暮らす　**b.** ～と平和活動をする　**c.** ～と和解する

B. 上の5つの文は本文に登場するものです。これらの意味から考えて、**Guess What?** で立てた予想は正しいですか。間違っていれば、選び直しましょう。

FIRST READING

DL 78~81　CD 2-28 ~ CD 2-31

英文を読み、あとに続く問題に答えなさい。

❶ **"In Hollywood there is a superstition that a movie is art only if it ends badly and you'll win an Academy Award only if you direct a movie about misery or play someone miserable," says Lindsay Doran,** whose résumé runs from production executive to president of United Artists and now to independent producer. **She believes, however, that people should have mood-elevating movies.**

❷ **In order to find out what kind of movies make people happy, she analyzed box-office hits and critically acclaimed movies on the American Film Institute's lists of favorites.** Interestingly, she found that the lead character winning at the end of the movie is not the most important element. Although American movies specialize in stories of accomplishment, audiences don't really care about the accomplishments. **Actually, many of the most popular and elevating movies end in loss:** in *Star Wars*, Obiwan dies, in *Harry Potter and the Half-Blood Prince*, Dumbledore dies, and in *Casablanca* and *Titanic*, the lovers can't stay together.

❸ **What makes an audience happy is not the moment of victory but the moment afterwards when the winners share that victory with someone they love.** They care

●●英文を読む前に●●

1. 知っている単語に ☑ を入れる
2. 【半数以上知っている】
→英文を読み、知らない単語の意味を類推する
【半数以上わからない】
→単語の意味を辞書で調べてから英文を読む

- □ superstition
- □ to win
- □ Academy Award
- □ to direct
- □ misery / miserable
- □ résumé
- □ to run
- □ production executive
- □ president

United Artists ユナイテッド・アーティスツ（かつての大手映画配給会社）

- □ independent
- □ however
- □ to find out
- □ box-office hits
- □ critically
- □ acclaimed

the American Film Institute アメリカン・フィルム・インスティチュート（AFI）＝米映画の保存・振興を目的とする非営利団体

- □ favorite
- □ interestingly
- □ element
- □ to specialize in ~
- □ accomplishment
- □ audience
- □ to care about ~
- □ loss
- □ to stay together
- □ victory
- □ afterwards
- □ to share

about relationships and the positive resolution of those relationships. In *Dirty Dancing*, for instance, the victorious heroine leaps into the arms of her trainer at the end and after that she reconciles with her father. After the Karate Kid wipes out his opponent, he makes peace with him. At the end of *The King's Speech*, the king overcomes his stammering and then shares his victory with his wife, daughters, and the crowds cheering outside the palace. We then are told that he and his speech therapist remain friends for the rest of their lives.

❹ "The 'happy ending' might be about not winning," concludes Ms. Doran. "It is about finding something deeper that means more than victory."

- ☐ relationship
- ☐ positive
- ☐ for instance
- ☐ victorious
- ☐ heroine
- ☐ to leap
- ☐ trainer
- ☐ to reconcile with
- ☐ to wipe out
- ☐ opponent
- ☐ to overcome
- ☐ stammering
- ☐ crowd
- ☐ to cheer
- ☐ palace
- ☐ therapist
- ☐ to remain
- ☐ rest
- ☐ to conclude

Paragraph Reading

A. 第❶段落の太字の 2 つの文の内容として正しいものを選びましょう。

a. アカデミー賞を受賞した映画はハッピーエンドばかりだ。

b. 後味の悪い結末の映画は評価されるが、観客が求めるのは気持ちを明るくする映画だ。

c. ハリウッド映画には悲劇的な結末が多く、観客もそれを求めている。

B. 第❷段落の太字の 2 つの文の内容として正しいものを選びましょう。

a. ヒット作を調べたら、観客が高揚感を感じる映画はハッピーエンドだった。

b. ヒット作を調べたら、観客が高揚感を感じる映画は悲しい結末が多かった。

c. ヒット作を調べたら、観客が高揚感を感じる映画はハッピーエンドでも悲劇でもなかった。

C. 第❸段落の太字の文から、この段落の内容として正しいものを選びなさい。

a. 観客が幸せを感じるのは、勝者が愛する人と喜びを分かち合うシーンだ。

b. 観客が幸せを感じるのは、勝者のその後の成功を描いたシーンだ。

c. 観客が幸せを感じるのは、勝利のシーンだ。

SECOND READING

Close Reading 関係代名詞

太字の関係代名詞が修飾している部分を下線 A ～ C から選びましょう。

1. A happy ending (A) is about finding something (B) deeper (C) **that** means more than victory.

2. *Harry Potter* (A) is about a wizard boy (B) **who** fights against an evil wizard (C).

3. *Anne of Green Gables* (A) is about a girl (B) **whose** hair (C) is red.

POINT!

２つの文で同じ人物・事物が入っているときは、関係代名詞を使って同じ人物・事物を関連付けて１文にすることができます。英文を読むとき、関係代名詞の後に続く部分が、文のどの部分と関連付けられているのかを正しくとらえることが大切です。

主格	所有格	目的格
who（その人が）	whose（その人の）	whom（その人を）
which（その事物が）	whose（その事物の）	that / which（その事物を）
that（限定された事物が）	whose（限定された事物の）	that（限定された事物を）

1. "You'll only win an Academy Award if you direct a movie about misery," says Lindsay Doran. ⇒元になる文で、関連付ける単語は人物
2. Her [=Lindsay Doran's] résumé runs from production executive to president of United Artists Pictures. ⇒挿入する文で関連付ける単語は所有格

⬇

"You'll only win an Academy Award if you direct a movie about misery," says Lindsay Doran, **whose** résumé runs from production executive to president of United Artists Pictures and now to independent producer.（whose resumé ＝ドーランの履歴書）

Reading Comprehension

本文の内容に合う文はT、合わないものはFを選びましょう。

1. アカデミー賞を取る映画は、どれもハッピーエンドだ。 [T / F]

2. ハッピーエンドで終わる映画は必ずヒットする。 [T / F]

3. 観客を幸せな気持ちにさせる映画では、結末で良好な人間関係が築かれる。 [T / F]

Listening

DL 82 CD 2-32

①〜③の音声を聞き、それぞれの内容と合うものをa、bから選びましょう。

① **a.** アメリカの映画には偉業を達成する物語が特に多い。
b. アメリカの映画界は偉業を達成した。

② **a.** 勝利を得たヒロインは最後にトレーナーの腕の中へ飛び込んでいく。
b. 最後に、ヒロインはトレーナーの手助けによって勝利をつかむ。

③ **a.** 彼と彼のスピーチセラピストは残りの人生を友人たちと過ごした。
b. 彼と彼のスピーチセラピストはその後もずっと友人であり続けた。

① [ ] ② [ ] ③ [ ]

REFLECTION

Fill in the Blanks

DL 83 CD 2-33

本文の中に出てくる英文を聞き、空欄に語句を入れ文を完成させましょう。

1. ( ) ( ) an Academy Award only if you ( ) a movie about misery.

2. In order ( ) ( ) ( ) what kind of movies make people happy, she ( ) box-office hits.

3. In *Casablanca* and *Titanic*, the lovers ( ) ( ) ( ).

Writing & Speaking

A. ①～⑤は映画のタイトルです。①～⑤の映画のジャンルをA～Eから選びましょう。

Movie Titles	Genre
① *Friday the 13th*	**A.** action-adventure film
② *Spider-Man*	**B.** fantasy film
③ *Harry Potter and the Sorcerer's Stone*	**C.** horror film
④ *Roman Holiday*	**D.** romance film
⑤ *E.T. the Extra-Terrestrial*	**E.** sci-fi (science fiction) film

① [　　] ② [　　] ③ [　　] ④ [　　] ⑤ [　　]

B. 今度は①～⑤の映画の内容を表すものを右から選び、線で結びましょう。

① *Friday the 13th* •	• Children help an alien go back to his planet.
② *Spider-Man* •	• A wizard boy fights against an evil wizard.
③ *Harry Potter and the Sorcerer's Stone* •	• Jason murders one camper after another.
④ *Roman Holiday* •	• A superhero fights to save the world.
⑤ *E.T. the Extra-Terrestrial* •	• A princess falls in love with a journalist.

C. AとBの表現を使い、例にならって関係代名詞を使い、4つの映画のジャンルと内容を1文で説明しましょう。

① (例) *Friday the 13th* is a horror film, **in which** Jason murders one camper after another.

② *Spider-Man* ______________________, ______________________

____.

③ *Harry Potter and the Sorcerer's Stone* ______________________, ____________

____.

④ *Roman Holiday* ______________________, ______________________

____.

⑤ *E.T. the Extra-Terrestrial* ______________________, ____________

____.

Unit 14 Beyond the Milky Way: *What the Stars Tell Us*

LET'S START!

Guess What?

"Beyond the Milky Way: *What the Stars Tell Us*" というタイトルから何に関する文章を予想しますか。

a. 天体観測からわかる宇宙の大きさ

b. 牧場の牛乳売りの話

c. 天の川と七夕にまつわる話

Check Words

A. 下線部の単語または語句の品詞に注意して、その意味を a ～ c から選びましょう。

1. Our solar system is part of a system of many stars − the Milky Way, our galaxy.
a. 銀河　**b.** 銀河のような　**c.** 星

2. In 1912 there was a breakthrough.　**a.** ～を通って　**b.** 大崩壊　**c.** 大発見

3 Henrietta Leavitt, a young woman who was working at the Harvard College Observatory, invented a method of measuring the size of the cosmos.
a. 宇宙の大きさ　**b.** 花の大きさ　**c.** 宇宙が大きい

4. Cepheid stars vary in brightness with a fixed rhythm of a few days to a few months.
a. 明るい　**b.** 明るさ　**c.** 明るくする

5. The Hubble Space Telescope has beamed back extremely sharp images of galaxies billions of light years away.

a. 僅かな年月で　**b.** 光の年齢　**c.** 光年

B. 上の 5 つの文は本文に登場するものです。これらの意味から考えて、**Guess What?** で立てた予想は正しいですか。間違っていれば、選び直しましょう。

FIRST READING

DL 84~89　CD 2-34 ~ CD 2-39

英文を読み、あとに続く問題に答えなさい。

❶ Since Galileo's time, telescopes have become increasingly bigger and better, enabling astronomers to explore further and further into the sky in order to broaden our understanding of the universe.

❷ In the 1700s it was found that our solar system is part of a system of many stars—the Milky Way, our galaxy. Then in 1781 Charles Messier saw what appeared to be clouds, which he called nebulae. This led to a great debate: Were these nebulae within our galaxy or were they separate galaxies?

❸ In 1912 there was a breakthrough. Henrietta Leavitt, a young woman who was working at the Harvard College Observatory, invented a method of measuring the size of the cosmos. Here is how she did it.

❹ It was known that so-called Cepheid stars vary in brightness with a fixed rhythm of a few days to a few months. Leavitt noticed that if two Cepheid stars have the same variation period, they have a similar brightness. Also, if one appears fainter, it is farther away. Her discovery allowed the famous astronomer Edwin Hubble to prove that a Cepheid variable star in the Andromeda Nebula was far beyond the Milky Way. And that led to the stunning realization

●●英文を読む前に●●

1. 知っている単語に ☑ を入れる
2. 【半数以上知っている】
　→英文を読み、知らない単語の意味を類推する
　【半数以上わからない】
　→単語の意味を辞書で調べてから英文を読む

□ telescope
□ increasingly
□ to enable
□ astronomer
□ to explore
□ further
□ in order to do
□ to broaden
□ understanding
□ universe
□ solar system
□ to appear to do
□ cloud
nebulae 星雲（nebula）の複数形
□ debate
□ to separate
□ observatory
□ to invest
□ method
□ to measure
□ so-called
Cepheid star ケフェウス変光星
□ to vary
□ to notice
variation period 明るさを変化させる一定の周期。周期と明るさに関連がある。
□ similar
□ discovery
□ to prove
□ the Andromeda
□ the Milky Way
□ stunning
□ realization

that the universe is full of galaxies.

❺ Next, using one of the biggest telescopes ever built, Hubble charted the distance of the galaxies and was able to calculate that the universe must have exploded from a single point in space. That moment, about 13.7 billion years ago, is now called the Big Bang.

❻ **Today astronomers can see even deeper into the universe than ever with the Hubble Space Telescope, named after this outstanding astronomer.** Orbiting around Earth, it has beamed back extremely sharp images of galaxies billions of light years away. The next step in astronomy will be to discover planets with life, perhaps intelligent life.

- □ full of ~
- □ telescope
- □ ever
- □ to chart
- □ distance
- □ to calculate
- □ to explode
- □ the Big Bang
- □ to name after ~
- □ outstanding
- □ to orbit
- □ Earth
- □ to beam
- □ extremely
- □ astronomy
- □ perhaps
- □ intelligent

Paragraph Reading

A. 第❶段落の太字の文の内容として、正しいものを選びましょう。

a. 望遠鏡の性能の向上とともに宇宙の理解が深まった。

b. ガリレオは望遠鏡のサイズを大きくし、宇宙の研究をした。

c. ガリレオ時代の天文学者は望遠鏡を使わないで遠くの宇宙を観測した。

B. 第❸段落の太字の２つの文の内容として、正しいものを選びましょう。

a. ある大発見をきっかけに、リービットは宇宙を観測する方法を考案した。

b. リービットはその大発見をした当時、ハーバード大学の天文台で無給で働いていた。

c. リービットは宇宙の大きさを測る方法を発見した。

C. 第❻段落の太字の文の内容として、正しいものを選びましょう。

a. ハッブル宇宙望遠鏡はより遠くの宇宙を見ることができるようにとハッブルの名前にあやかって名付けられた。

b. 今日の天文学者は宇宙に設置された望遠鏡を使ってより遠くの星を眺めることができる。

c. 今日、天文学者はハッブル宇宙望遠鏡を使ってこれまで以上に宇宙についてより深く知ることができる。

SECOND READING

Close Reading 比較級

英文の下線部の意味を a、b から選びましょう。

1. If one appears fainter, it is farther away.

   a. 一方（の星）がより光が弱ければ　b. 一方（の星）がより速く消えれば

2. Today astronomers can see even deeper into the universe than ever with the Hubble Space Telescope.

   a. 天文学者はこれまで以上に深い場所から宇宙を観察することができる

   b. 天文学者はこれまで以上に宇宙の奥深くを見ることができる

POINT!

何かを比較するときは形容詞・副詞の比較級を使います。たいていは than を用いて「～よりも～だ」という意味を表します。

比較級の変化

❶単音節の形容詞・副詞＝形容詞・副詞＋ er

（例）smaller / longer / older

Our garden is smaller than yours.（私たちの庭はあなたの庭よりも小さい）

❷二音節以上の形容詞・副詞＝ more ＋形容詞・副詞

（例）more important / more beautiful / more useful

The fact is more important than the opinion.（事実は意見よりも大事です）

❸不規則変化

（例）good → better / bad → worse / little → less

Six is less than nine.（6 は 9 よりも少ない〈小さい〉）

Reading Comprehension

本文の内容に合う文はT、合わないものはFを選びましょう。

1. メシエによる星雲の発見は、大きな議論を巻き起こした。 [T / F]

2. 宇宙は多くの銀河で満ちている。 [T / F]

3. ハッブル宇宙望遠鏡を使えば、何百億光年先まで宇宙を観測できる。 [T / F]

Listening

DL 90 CD 2-40

①〜③の音声を聞き、それぞれの内容と合うものをa、bから選びましょう。

① **a.** 1781年、メシエは雲のように見えるものを星雲と名付けた。
b. 1781年、メシエは雲の上にある星雲を発見した。

② **a.** それにより、天の川と呼ばれる銀河が発見された。
b. それにより、宇宙は数多くの銀河に満ちているという素晴らしい事実がわかった。

③ **a.** 13.7億年前のまさにこの瞬間に、それはビッグ・バンと呼ばれるようになった。
b. 137億年前のその瞬間は、今ではビッグ・バンと呼ばれている。

① [ ] ② [ ] ③ [ ]

REFLECTION

Fill in the Blanks

DL 91 CD 2-41

本文の中に出てくる英文を聞き、空欄に語句を入れ文を完成させましょう。

1. ( ) Galileo's time, telescopes have become ( ) and ( ).

2. ( ) these nebulae ( ) our galaxy or were they ( ) galaxies?

3. Using ( ) ( ) the ( ) telescopes ( ) built, he charted the distance of the galaxies.

Writing & Speaking

A. 本文では know / notice / prove / calculate といった that 節を伴う動詞が使われています。これらの【動詞 + that 節】を用いて、日本語に合うように①～③の英文を完成させましょう。

	誰が	どうする	何を（に）
（例）	Messier （メシエは）	noticed （気づいた）	there were nebulae in the sky （空に星雲がある）
①	（私は）	（知っている）	my sister is kind （妹が優しい）
②	（彼女は）	（証明した）	this circle is bigger than that one （この円はあの円よりも大きい）
③	（彼は）	（計算した）	it took one hour to reach the station （駅へ着くのに 1 時間かかった）

（例）Messier noticed that there were nebulae in the sky.
（メシエは空に星雲があることに気づいた）

① ______________________________

____

② ______________________________

____

③ ______________________________

____

B. ペアを組み、①～③について A さんは日本語を言い、B さんはそれに相当する英語を言いましょう。終わったら役割を交代して練習しましょう。

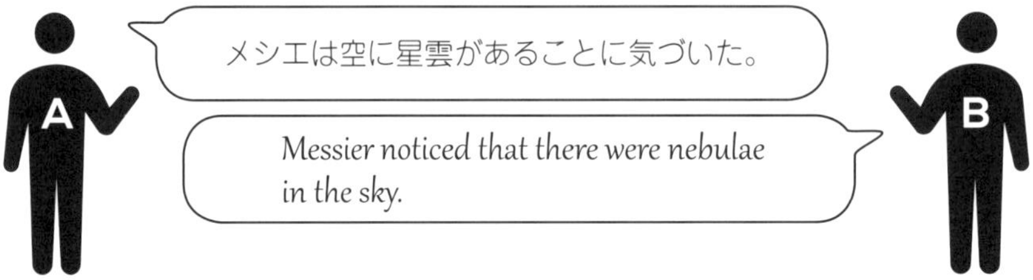

Unit 15 Zahra's Paradise: *Telling the World about Iran*

LET'S START!

Guess What?

"Zahra's Paradise: *Telling the World about Iran*" というタイトルから何に関する文章を予想しますか。

a. イランのザフラーという神話の話

b. ザフラーがイランにある娯楽施設を紹介する話

c.「ザフラーの楽園」の作者がイランの情勢を伝える話

Check Words

A. 下線部の単語または語句の品詞に注意して、その意味をa～cから選びましょう。

1. Iran is a theocracy, a form of government based on religion and controlled by religious leaders. **a.** 論理的な **b.** 神学 **c.** 神権政治

2. University students began protesting. **a.** 妨げる **b.** 抗議 **c.** 防衛

3. The proponents called their protest the Green Revolution.
a. 革命 **b.** 回転 **c.** 変化した

4. Twitter and other social-networking sites enabled the protesters to communicate.
a. 抗議する人々が～することを妨げる
b. 抗議する人々に～することを強制する
c. 抗議する人々が～することを可能にする

5. To make a comic like this, only a pencil and imagination are needed.
a. 漫画 **b.** 小説 **c.** おもしろい

B. 上の5つの文は本文に登場するものです。これらの意味から考えて、**Guess What?** で立てた予想は正しいですか。間違っていれば、選び直しましょう。

FIRST READING

DL 92~94 CD 2-42 ~ CD 2-44

英文を読み、あとに続く問題に答えなさい。

❶ **Amir left Iran when he was 11 years old. Like many Iranians abroad, he is an exile who opposes the present government of Iran.** Iran is a theocracy, a form of government based on religion and controlled by religious leaders. It wasn't always that way in Iran. It used to be ruled by a king called a shah. In 1977 the shah was overthrown, and the Islamic Republic of Iran was born. Iranians looked forward to a new era. However, many people were disappointed with the results.

❷ **In the big 2009 presidential election the government's candidate won although the opposition candidate had the most votes. University students began protesting.** Soon hundreds of thousands of people joined the anti-government rallies. This led to a violent conflict between the government and the demonstrators. The protest then went underground and continued overseas. The protestors called their movement the Green Revolution, reflecting the campaign color of the opposition candidate. The protest is also called the "Twitter Revolution" because Twitter and other social-networking sites enabled the protesters to communicate.

❸ **Amir started a comic-web to tell the world about the protests.** He named it *Zahra's Paradise* after a cemetery in Teheran.

●●英文を読む前に●●

1. 知っている単語に ☑ を入れる
2. 【半数以上知っている】→英文を読み、知らない単語の意味を類推する
【半数以上わからない】→単語の意味を辞書で調べてから英文を読む

- ☐ to leave
- ☐ abroad
- ☐ exile
- ☐ to oppose
- ☐ present
- ☐ government
- ☐ form
- ☐ religion / religious
- ☐ to rule
- ☐ to overthrow

Islamic Republic of Iran
イラン・イスラム共和国（イランの正式名称）

- ☐ to look forward to ~
- ☐ era
- ☐ disappointed
- ☐ result
- ☐ presidential election
- ☐ candidate
- ☐ opposition candidate
- ☐ vote
- ☐ hundreds of thousands of ~
- ☐ to join
- ☐ anti-
- ☐ rally
- ☐ conflict
- ☐ demonstrator
- ☐ to continue
- ☐ overseas
- ☐ movement
- ☐ to reflect
- ☐ campaign
- ☐ to communicate
- ☐ cemetery

It's the story of a mother whose son vanished in the protests of 2009. To depict this story, Amir took the images that bloggers were sending out of Iran. He says that it was the collective effort of a Jewish editor, an Arab artist, and an Iranian author (himself). In Iran such a journalist would have his camera taken away, but to make a comic like this, only a pencil and imagination are needed. "The idea that Iranian people have been silenced is totally wrong," he says.

- ☐ to vanish
- ☐ to depict
- ☐ blogger
- ☐ to send
- ☐ collective
- ☐ effort
- ☐ Jewish
- ☐ editor
- ☐ Arab
- ☐ author
- ☐ to take away
- ☐ imagination
- ☐ to silence
- ☐ wrong

Zahra's Paradise は書籍化もされ、オランダやスペイン、イタリアなど 10 数カ国で翻訳されている。

Paragraph Reading

A. 第❶段落の太字の 2 つの文の内容として、正しいものを選びましょう。

a. アミールは家族の反対を押し切って国外に逃亡した。

b. アミールはイラン人の慣習として 11 歳になるとイランを離れた。

c. アミールはイランの政治体制に反対して亡命した。

B. 第❷段落の太字の 2 つの文の内容として、正しいものを選びましょう。

a. 2009 年の大統領選挙はお祭り騒ぎとなり、多くの人々が関心を示した。

b. 2009 年の大統領選挙では、対立政党が得票数の再集計を求めた。

c. 2009 年の大統領選挙で選出方法に疑義があり、大学生たちが抗議した。

C. 第❸段落の太字の文の内容として、正しいものを選びましょう。

a. アミールはウェブサイト上に漫画を書くことで世間に抗議した。

b. アミールは抗議の件を世間に伝えるため漫画のウェブサイトを始めた。

c. アミールがウェブサイト上で書いた漫画は世界中から非難された。

SECOND READING

Close Reading 不定詞

英文の下線部の意味を a、b から選びましょう。

1. Amir started a comic-web <u>to tell the world</u> about the protests.

a. 世に知らせるために

b. 世に知らせること

2. <u>To depict this story</u>, Amir took the images that bloggers were sending out of Iran.

a. この話を描写すること

b. この話を描写するために

POINT!

不定詞は、名詞・形容詞・副詞の働きをする動詞の形です。

形	to ＋動詞の原形
用法	①名詞的用法（～すること） I like **to jog** on the beach. （私は砂浜でジョギングすることが好きだ） ②形容詞的用法（～するための） Give me something **to write** with. （何か書くものをください） ③副詞的用法（～するために） I called her **to tell** her the truth. （本当のことを知らせるために彼女に電話した）

Reading Comprehension

本文の内容に合う文は T、合わないものは F を選びましょう。

1. イランはイスラム教に基づきイスラム教の指導者によって管理される政治体制である。 [T / F]
2. 抗議する人々はツイッターなどの SNS を通じてコミュニケーションをとった。 [T / F]
3. 漫画を書くためには、ペンと携帯だけがあればよい。 [T / F]

Listening

DL 95　CD 2-45

①〜③の音声を聞き、それぞれの内容と合うものを a、b から選びましょう。

① **a.** イランの人々は新世界を遠くに見た。
b. イランの人々は新しい時代を待ち望んだ。

② **a.** 抗議する人々の運動は、野党のキャンペーンカラーにちなんで「緑の革命」と呼ばれた。
b. 抗議する人々は環境に配慮する人々が多かったため、抗議運動は「緑の革命」と呼ばれた。

③ **a.** 彼は、漫画はユダヤ人、アラブ人そしてイラン人のためのものだと述べた。
b. 彼は、漫画はユダヤ人編集者、アラブ人の芸術家そしてイラン人の著者の共同作業だと述べた。

① [　　] ② [　　] ③ [　　]

REFLECTION

Fill in the Blanks

DL 96　CD 2-46

本文の中に出てくる英文を聞き、空欄に語句を入れ文を完成させましょう。

1. A theocracy is a (　　　　) of government based on (　　　　) and controlled by (　　　　) leaders.
2. Twitter and other (　　　　)-networking (　　　　) enabled the protesters (　　) (　　　　).
3. Amir (　　　　) a comic-web Zahra's Paradise (　　　　) a cemetery in Teheran.

Writing & Speaking

A. 本文で使われた「～することを楽しみにする」を意味する look forward to と、「～と言う」を意味する say that の表現を用いて、日本語に合うように①～④の英文を完成させましょう。

	誰が	look forward to	何を
（例）	We （私たちは）	〈現在進行形〉	this weekend （今週末）
①	（彼は）	〈現在進行形〉	（スキーシーズン）
②	（彼女たちは）	〈過去形〉	（ビーチへ行くこと）

	誰が	say that	何を
（例）	She （彼女は）	〈現在形〉	it's an old book. （それは古い本だ）
③	（彼は）	〈過去形〉	（納豆が好きだ）
④	（私の祖父は）	〈過去形〉	（いつかイランへ行きたい）

（例）We are looking forward to this weekend. / She says that it's an old book.
（私たちは今週末を楽しみにしている）（彼女はそれが古い本だと言う）

① ______________________________

____

② ______________________________

____

③ ______________________________

____

④ ______________________________

____

B. ペアを組み、①～④について A さんは日本語を言い、B さんはそれに相当する英語を言いましょう。終わったら役割を交代して練習しましょう。

不規則動詞　活用表

テキストで扱った不規則動詞の活用をまとめた一覧です。

原形（意味）	過去形	過去分詞形
am, is（～である）	was	been
are（～である）	were	been
bear（～を産む）	bore	borne, born
beat（～を打つ）	beat	beaten, beat
become（～になる）	became	become
begin（～を始める）	began	begun
blow（吹く）	blew	blown
break（～を壊す）	broke	broken
bring（～を持ってくる）	brought	brought
build（～を建てる）	built	built
burn（燃える）	burnt, burned	burnt, burned
buy（～を買う）	bought	bought
come（来る）	came	come
cost（～〔金〕がかかる）	cost	cost
cut（～を切る）	cut	cut
do / does（～をする）	did	done
drink（～を飲む）	drank	drunk
eat（～を食べる）	ate	eaten
fall（落ちる）	fell	fallen
feed（～に食べ物を与える）	fed	fed
feel（～を感じる）	felt	felt
find（～を見つける）	found	found
get（～を得る）	got	got, gotten
give（～を与える）	gave	given
go（行く）	went	gone
grow（成長する）	grew	grown
have / has（～を持っている）	had	had
hear（～が聞こえる）	heard	heard

hit（～を打つ）	hit	hit
hold（～を持つ）	held	held
know（～を知っている）	knew	known
lead（～を導く）	led	led
leap（はねる）	leaped, leapt	leaped, leapt
leave（～を去る）	left	left
make（～を作る）	made	made
overcome（～に打ち勝つ）	overcame	overcome
overthrow（～をくつがえす）	overthrew	overthrown
put（～を置く）	put	put
read（～を読む） [ri:d] 発音のみ変化	read [red]	read [red]
rise（のぼる）	rose	risen
run（走る）	ran	run
say（言う）	said	said
see（～を見る）	saw	seen
sell（～を売る）	sold	sold
send（～を送る）	sent	sent
shine（光る）	shone, shined	shone, shined
shoot（打つ）	shot	shot
sink（沈む）	sank, sunk	sunk, sunken
spend（～を費やす）	spent	spent
stand（立つ、～を立たせる）	stood	stood
take（～を〔手に〕取る）	took	taken
tell（～を話す）	told	told
think（～と思う）	thought	thought
throw（～を投げる）	threw	thrown
wear（～を着ている）	wore	worn
win（～に勝つ）	won	won
write（～を書く）	wrote	written

本書には音声 CD（別売）があります

A New Look at the World

—Easy to Read Contemporary Topics—

英語リーディング入門 新たな世界を開く 15 章

2020 年 1 月 20 日　初版第 1 刷発行
2023 年 2 月 20 日　初版第 5 刷発行

著　者　原田　祐貨
橋本　健広
Patricia Massy

発行者　福岡　正人
発行所　株式会社　**金星堂**
（〒 101-0051）東京都千代田区神田神保町 3-21
Tel. (03) 3263-3828（営業部）
(03) 3263-3997（編集部）
Fax (03) 3263-0716
http://www.kinsei-do.co.jp

編集担当　長島吉成　Printed in Japan
印刷所・製本所／三美印刷株式会社

ISBN978-4-7647-4104-1　C1082